# Soviets

"It is a very good idea to record history through the lens. History in photos is clear and comprehensible. No painter can depict on canvas what the camera sees."

—V. I. Lenin

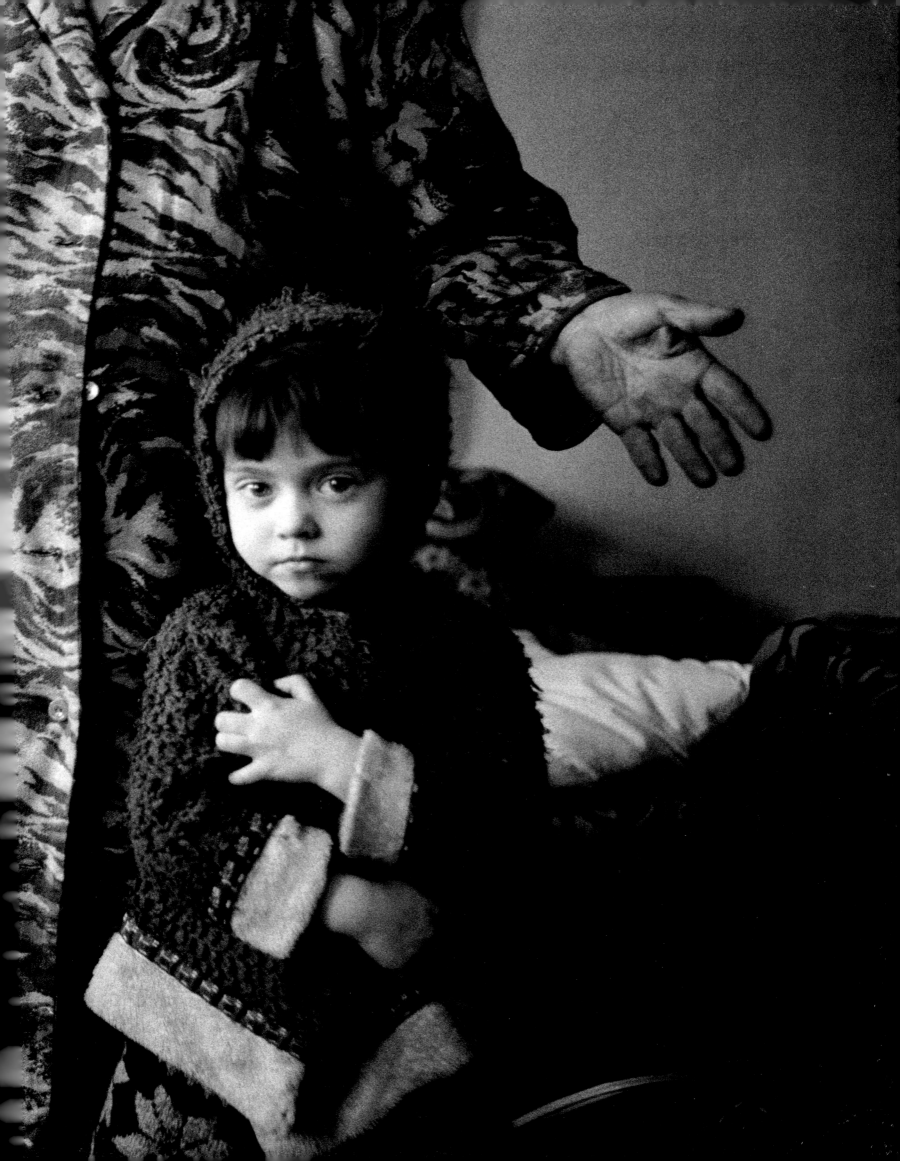

| РЕЙС | АЭРОПОРТ ОТПРАВЛЕНИЯ | ВРЕМ ПО РАСПИ |
|---|---|---|
| 6666 | 1ЯКТЫБЭК66666666 | 66 |
| 6666 | Л9-666662Е | КО |
| 8ЫЫ8 | 310ША1ИХД ЯЯРЖ_ | 7Б |
| 39ВШ | БАЛКЭ ЦДБХ/6Н.И- | ЭД |
| ФОlБ | ЛЧЗВ86АС2ЛЬШЫ/А | БК |
| ЧЭ0Л | ЧПИГ8765LТХШ7Р5Ш | ИЧ |
| ВЗПМ | ЯЛБЧТАРЧ0ГГБЗБ | МО |
| ЦШТ7 | 1Ш_ЦНШД0Я ШЯХМФ | Б/ |
| /ЯШL | КLЗИТСЛ0ГАЛДШШФУ | Ш Г |
| Э"ЧЛ | ЕЧФСКБ8L ЬЧЬСТЦ3 | 19 |
|  | Л5ФЮА7ЮL ЧСЛИЯН- | ЗА |
| FЕЛЖ | ЗА 8ЧУ5 6ТЬ-ИЛК | 8l |
| ЧАКЫ | КУРЧЦВКF КЧЗЧЕЕЮ | КУ |
| СРРУ | ИУУРРКЮЧ ККШС69Г | ХР |
| ЛЮИУ | ИИИ-РИЮL Ч7РЮТАУ | И- |

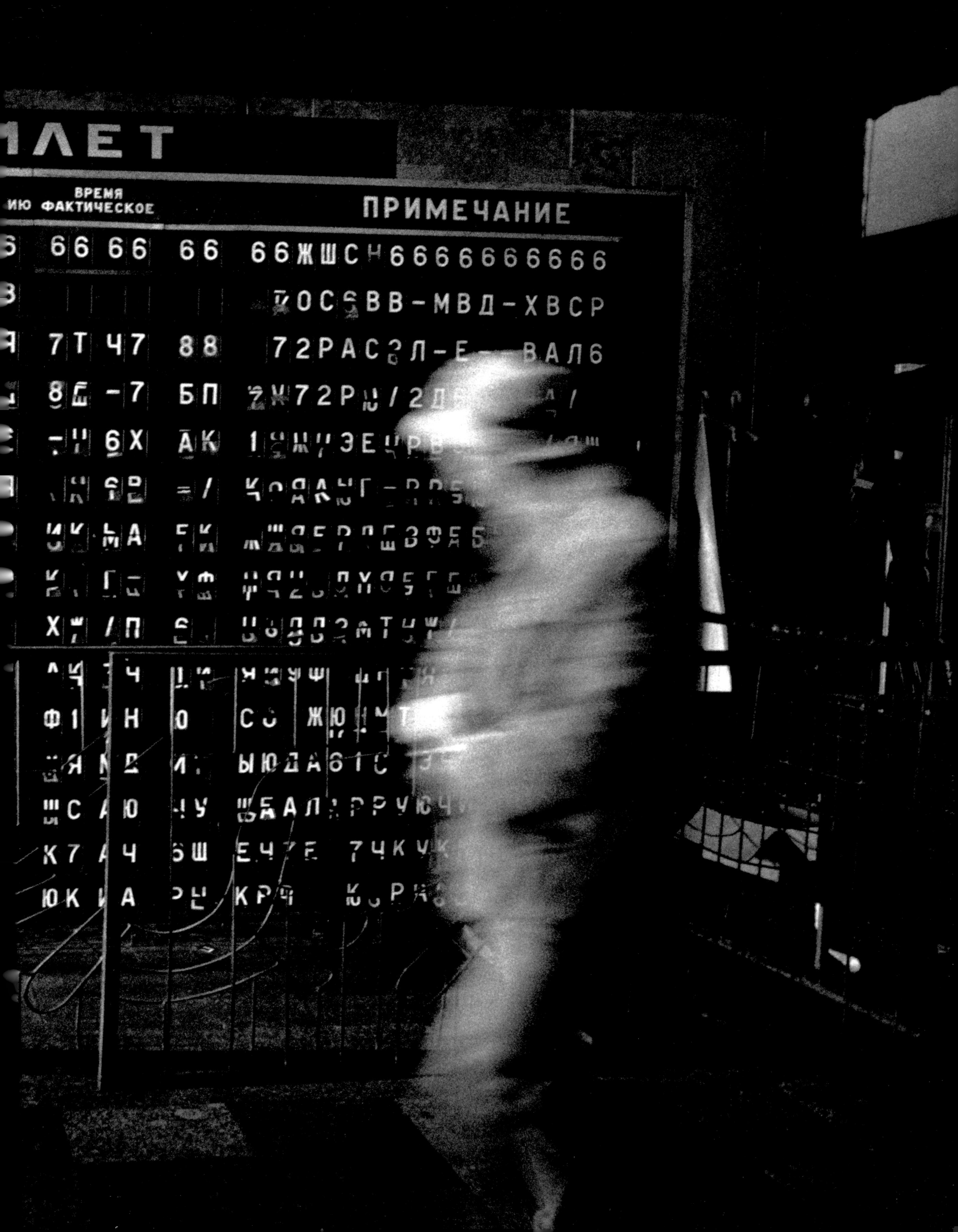
ВРЕМЯ
ФАКТИЧЕСКОЕ
ПРИМЕЧАНИЕ

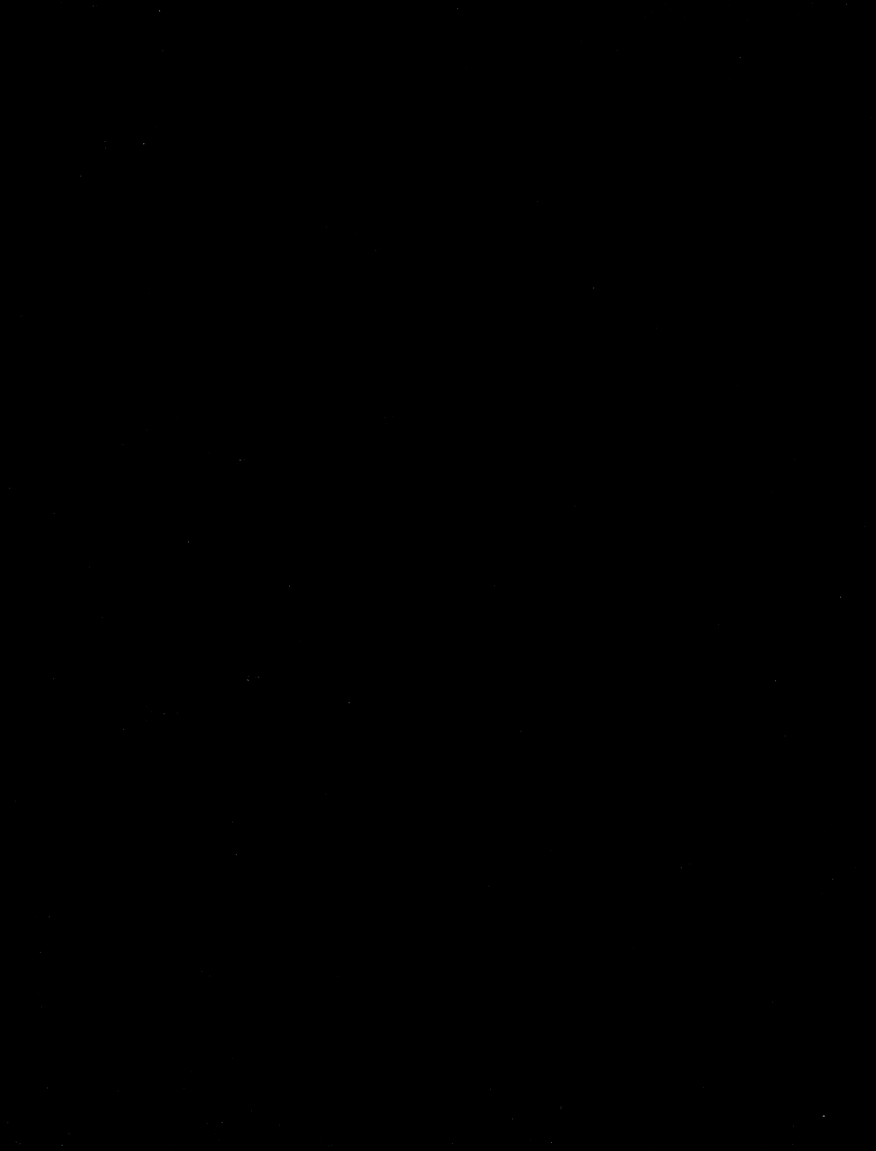

Shepard Sherbell

# SOVIETS

## Pictures from the End of the USSR

Foreword by Serge Schmemann

Yale University Press  New Haven and London

Preceding illustrations

1

**MARCH 1991, Novokuznyetsk (Stalinsk), Kuzbass region, Siberia** *Babushka*
complains that while her granddaughter's parents are working in the coal mine all day, she
has no running water and has to walk a half mile each way to fetch some and she's too old
for that and the heat goes off half the day and the roof is leaking and now, with the miners
on strike, there is not enough money to buy food in the private shops and the state shops
sell bad meat and what can the foreigner do about it besides take her picture? Nobody
realizes that this miner's strike will set the wheels in motion for the collapse of the Soviet
Union in just eight months' time.

2

**MARCH 1991, Tiraspol, Moldova** In the Political Office of the Supreme Soviet,
Transdniester Moldovan Republic, a Russian-speaking breakaway region from Romanian-
speaking Moldova. Today is Referendum Day, and the people will again express their wish
for independence. No one, pointedly not even Russia, has recognized this "state" to date,
preferring that it settle its differences peacefully with the Moldovans. General Alexander I.
Lebed ("First we will act, then we will explain"), hero of the Afghanistan war and commander
of the 14th Soviet Army camped nearby, hopes that his mere presence will prevent hasty
or ill-considered actions by either side.

3

**JUNE 1992** The flight announcement board was imported at great expense from Italy
seven years ago for the Mari Airport Terminal, near the market town of Turkmenistan's Kara
Kum Desert Region. The board has never worked; it probably was damaged in shipment,
and nobody knows how to fix it. What it does do, however, is to flip over Cyrillic letters
randomly every few seconds. The airport manager left it in place, plugged it in, and had a
delicate but patriotic wrought-iron fence built around it. Waiting for my flight to Ashkabad,
I'm spellbound by a random-poetry machine that the Russian avant-gardists of the 1920s
would have loved.

4

**MARCH 1992, Moscow** A mother in Manezh Square, near the Kremlin. She is protest-
ing the disappearance of her son, a conscript who served in Afghanistan. He has been
missing more than four years, since the Soviet Army pulled out in 1988–89. She is a mem-
ber of *Nadezhda* ("Hope"), modeled on the Mothers of the Plaza de Mayo in Argentina.
Nadezhda started demonstrating in the late 1980s, when it was potentially dangerous, and
continues now, when it is utterly futile.

Soviet troops returning from the Afghanistan war were thought of in their own country
as drug-addled, untrustworthy pariahs. The veterans finally achieved the public respect they
had been denied when, at the outset of the August 1991 putsch, hundreds came unbidden
to the Russian Parliament to defend it against the plotters. They built and manned barri-
cades of wooden bench slats and iron fences. Many said this was their chance to strike a
blow against the kind of hardliners who had sent them to Afghanistan.

5

**MAY 1992** A roadside scene near Dushanbe, Tajikistan. Many rural Soviets treat the
family cow as a pet, albeit a productive and valuable one.

# Contents

Captions for the photographs appear at the end of each section

# Foreword by Serge Schmemann

These pictures are stark, black and white, unsentimental. You will find no gingerbread churches here, no grandiose palaces, no log houses listing quaintly among birches in early spring. Yet the memories they bring back are curiously deep, and not all bleak. It is *this* Soviet Union, *this* Russia in which people really lived and live—and in which I also lived for ten years. Yes, of course we visited the Kremlin, gazed in awe on the fabulous icons, marveled at the palaces of old St. Petersburg reflected in the great Neva. But that Russia was a museum to a past the Soviets butchered and then fixed in the formaldehyde of their invented history. The actual world the Soviet state created was one of these images: ugly blocks of badly built housing, crude factories spewing poisons, a system designed everywhere to serve the state, whatever the cost to people, nature, or the future.

Yet it is in these settings that human dignity is truly tested, and it is here that the memories turn poignant. Look at the people in these pictures: they have not all been crushed; far from it. Look at the eyes of the mother holding a picture of her son, missing in Afghanistan. Look at the smile of the woman leading her cow past a statue of a worker. Look at the satisfaction of the truck driver who has devised a bath on a bleak Kuril Island. And even in the worst of places, the labor camp for young women in Ryazan, look at the face of the warden. These are deeply human faces, a humanity that not only has survived war, slavery, murder, poverty, and harsh labor, but perhaps has been honed by it.

These pictures are not pretty. But I know that old woman standing over the stove in a communal apartment in her tattered housedress, old apron, and well-worn felt *tufli,* the slippers into which everyone changes on entering the house. I also know how rude it is not to accept a pair and to keep my own shoes on, however squeamish I might feel, just as I know you never keep your coat on past the entryway. Most Russians are only one generation removed from the countryside, where there were good reasons to keep felt boots and crude sheepskin outerwear out of the cramped log house after a day of work. I recognize the rags, tins, and assorted belongings stuffed in every crack. I've been in this *communalka*—in Moscow, Kostroma, Tula, Irkutsk, Yakutsk, Vladivostok, in countless villages and towns. I know the smell, of boiling cabbage, drying laundry, crude detergent, cheap tobacco, frying onions, tired bodies; I know the sound, of hissing teapot, cursing neighbors, playing children, passing trucks, the oversized television set that is always left on, though the picture has long gone green.

I know her life is unbearably hard, that she may share her room with a married daughter and a grandchild, that the families in the other rooms fight and drink, that kids put on galoshes to use the one bathroom, that on weekends she must board the *elektrichka,* the commuter train that will take her to a small plot of dirt where she will put in potatoes, just in case.

Yet I also know that she will invite me in, that she will offer me what she can—some tea, biscuits with homemade raspberry preserves on a small side-plate, maybe boiled potatoes with sunflower oil, sauerkraut, marinated mushrooms. I know the conversation will be about real things—memories of far harder times, the grandson lost in Afghanistan, questions about whether there is religion in my world.

I know that the time spent in that kitchen, in that black-and-white world that Shepard Sherbell has captured, will stay with me forever. It is where I learned about the avarice and cruelty of unconstrained state power, and it is where I discovered the enormous capacity of the human spirit to persevere. Not everyone, of course, perhaps not even most. The victims are here too—the young prisoners whose eyes reflect nothing any more; the corpses of people felled by despair, alcohol, war, bad medicine; the workers who will die of blackened lungs and poisoned blood.

These pictures are not sentimental. It is difficult to look at the old woman who drank acetic acid, at the oil pouring out of a tap, at the man peddling his belongings in Tallinn. Why should we, anyway? The Soviet Union is no more; the Moldovans, Georgians, Tajiks pictured here are free of Moscow's domination. The Russians can build their own future.

We need to know this world, of course, because it was, because our own lives in the West were shaped for so many years by the existential struggle with this same state. These factories were built and these people were twisted in a campaign to overcome us and what we stood for.

But we should also look on this because it still exists. The former Soviet world has changed greatly in the years since Communism caved in, but its legacy is awesome and deep. There are still far, far more similarities than differences between the Soviet Union and the struggling states it left behind. And for generations to come, the people of the former Soviet world will still be laboring under the legacies of that awesome, terrible experiment in socialist Utopia that was the Union of Soviet Socialist Republics.

Now, when the former Soviet republics all suffer from bankruptcy, corruption, and political confusion, when Russians and many of their neighbors find comfort in bringing back Communist leaders and idealizing the past, when we in the West try to make sense of a confusing world no longer neatly divided into empires of good and evil, we simply lack the remove to appreciate the full significance of that Soviet Union. Every corner of the globe was touched by the Soviet state and its ideology, whether through the murderous controls of the political police within the Union, or the loathing that the godless Big Brother and his militarized minions spread through America and Europe, or the allure that the Marxist vision of equality and perfectibility exerted on newly minted governments in the third world. No other country ever lost so many men in defense of its land, or killed so many of its own in the reckless pursuit of power and might. No other state ever succeeded in imposing so strict a control over the lives and thoughts of its subjects for so long.

I often wonder if people several generations from now will believe that there was such a place, a vast state conceived by idealists and born in revolution which attempted nothing less than to create an entirely new world and an entirely new being, an ideal creature stripped of greed, selfishness, superstition, aggressiveness, and tribalism; living only to serve the People. Karl Marx would never have thought that Russia would become the test tube for his ideas, but in retrospect it is possible to understand why it was that this huge land straddling two continents and peopled by many distinct nations would plunge into so formidable a folly.

It was a nation with an enormous chasm between the very rich and the very poor, a peasantry reared in communal villages, and a people that had always placed spirituality above practicality and always believed in a special destiny. From "Holy Russia" and the "Third Jerusalem" it was a natural leap to the Dictatorship of the Proletariat, as it was from an all-powerful autocrat to "all power to the Soviets." The greatest Russian leaders, those who came to be styled "the Great" or "the Terrible" ("stern" is a more accurate translation of Ivan's sobriquet), were simply those with the most audacious schemes and the fewest scruples. And when leaders came to power who could also claim to be of, for, and by the people, autocracy metamorphosed organically into totalitarianism. Only enemies of the State would argue with its leaders when the People rule. And who will mourn a few victims when a shining future beckons?

By 1980, when I arrived in Moscow, the system had settled into a dotage, exhausted by war, genocide, "personality cult," and simply old age. The old men who ran the system could only struggle to satisfy their all-devouring military and police machines, wringing the last drops of energy from a populace too battered to resist, or to work. "We pretend we work, you pretend you pay," was the guiding quip.

In that gray mood, so powerfully captured in the images of Shepard Sherbell, the marvel was not that there were so few rebels, but that there were any at all.

Look at the statues, the portraits of Lenin, the massive squares: everything was designed to extract fealty, to garnish the image of the omnipotent state, to crush any thought of defiance. It began at childhood—I remember my daughter returning from a few weeks of Kindergarten No. 18 and explaining that Lenin was the greatest man who ever lived. Look at the shelves in the shops, the dismal cafeterias: the distribution of every comfort and need big and small, from medical care to sausage, from the treasured Moscow living permit to a rare trip abroad, was parceled out in direct proportion to loyalty and usefulness. Informers were everywhere, even at home. And after the savagery of the Gulag, the very presumption of ubiquitous ears—signified by a silent finger pointed to the ceiling—was enough to instill fear and caution. The dissidents who became known to the West were either the truly desperate, people who had nothing left to lose and were awaiting either the labor camp or exile, or those sufficiently privileged, like Andrei Sakharov, that extraordinary measures were required to silence them. It is one of the many ironies of the fall of the Soviet Union that just before it went into its final decline, the KGB finally succeeded in imprisoning or exiling all the dissident groups that had sprouted in the "thaw" of the sixties and the promise of the Helsinki accords.

I will never forget my first month in Moscow as a correspondent, January 1980, when I witnessed the huge operation mounted to ship Sakharov into exile in Gorky. All telephone service in his region of Moscow was severed. KGB agents and cars were everywhere, and an entire Aeroflot jetliner was deployed to fly this one man out, all because he insisted that the Soviet state obey its own laws. Then came the Olympic games, dubbed by one journalist "hands across the metal detector." Entire army battalions were brought in to rebuild and repaint the city. Dissidents, children, and dogs were ordered out of Moscow, private cars were banned from much of the city, reserve officers were assigned stretches of street on which to be "passersby," ready to snatch a drunk or a pickpocket out of view of the foreign guests.

Yet even as the Soviet state rotted from within, so potent was the utopian allure of this ideology that leaders of newly independent states flocked to variations of its banner, creating a powerful block of countries that styled themselves "people's democracies," branded everyone else "imperialist," and piled up righteous resolutions in the United Nations. We may scorn that ideology now, yet not so long ago many in our own prosperous and smoothly functioning republic looked upon the spread of Communism with something akin to paranoia, hunting for commies at home and fighting wars to stop its contagion abroad.

In the end, it proved to be an experiment as monumental in its failure as it had been audacious in its presumption. The planned economy that was to do away with profit and greed created an elephantine bureaucracy and perpetrated some of the greatest ecological damage ever inflicted on our planet. The "new Soviet man" was often a drunkard or spectacularly corrupt. The promised land of peace and freedom became the world's most militarized and ruthless police state. And the "people's culture" became an anti-culture in which mediocrity was glorified and talent systematically crushed. Virtually every state that followed Moscow's lead, willingly or unwillingly, from China to Cuba and Estonia to Mozambique, was left stunted.

Surveying the ruins in these images, it is easy to be smug. In the epic struggle of our system and theirs, we won, and there are those who argue that there is no further reason to bother with Russia except to avoid "loose nukes." A new administration in Washington has made clear it wants no "special relationship" with Moscow, and prefers treating Russia as a Soviet Union stripped of empire and resources. In Moscow, President Vladimir Putin wants Russia taken seriously, and he wants to modernize it. But he is a low-ranking KGB agent with no experience of politics or rule of law, and the Russian economy is in terrible shape. Putin has brought some peace to the politics and economy, but he has mired Russia in the Chechen war, the oligarchs continue to plunder the economy, and the Kremlin is showing an ominous irritation with a free press.

But I believe that our fascination with Russia is not necessarily determined by political struggle. In the sentiments I feel as I leaf through this portfolio, I find myself still gripped by fascination with a people caught forever between greatness and failure, between East and West, between the heights of creativity and the depths of squalor. There is something awe inspiring in the capacity of the Russian people to survive. Somewhere back in time, perhaps under the Mongols, or under their warring princes, or under rapacious lords, invaders, and bosses, they learned that nothing is sure save the potatoes they themselves can grow, so long as they do not produce so many that others will become jealous or tempted. I remember when the lines began to grow long in the final days of Communism, and rationing was instituted, and people began to talk of economic reform, which in Russia has never meant anything but more misery, how many people—workers, scientists, composers—took their hoes, went outside the city, and began breaking up the sod for potatoes.

Despite all that, or perhaps because of it, the frozen Eurasian expanse continues to create remarkable poetry, music, and art. There are more theaters now in Moscow than there were under Soviet rule. The best of the underground writers have achieved world renown, and new cadres have taken their place in the thick Russian literary journals. Despite a constant tug of war over its ownership, Russian television provides a steady diet of fine documentaries.

I leaf through these images again. In many ways, they tell stories that language cannot. One of the problems of writing about Russia or the old Soviet Union is that the language that evolved there—the vocabulary of survival and fatalism, the brilliant gallows humor—is also the most difficult to export. Those who expressed it best—bards like the great Vladimir Vysotsky, whose songs were known to every Russian, or comedians like Arkady Raikin, who was allowed enormous liberties because he made even Politburo members laugh—are virtually unknown in the West, because so little of their work can be translated. Their language was a shorthand shaped by the street and the exigencies of eluding Big Brother. Vysotsky sang about the routine ordeals of Soviet life—veterans, queues, fears. Raikin's one-liners became instant aphorisms—"the doctors treated him and treated him, but he recovered."

Every facet of life had its lexicon. Shopping was expressed as scrounging—when things appeared in the stores they were "thrown out," because they were snatched up within minutes of appearing on the shelves. Nobody "bought" anything—they "took" them, because the issue was not price, or choice, but simply finding something. The collapse of Communism promised a reversal of the state of affairs—and that, Russians soon noted with their well-honed fatalism, is what happened. "No more taboos," a woman told me, "and no more food." New comedians quickly arose, the brilliant Mikhail Zhvanetsky first among them, to seize on the cruel ironies of the new order: "In the old days, it was impossible to live, but everybody did it anyway. Now, of course, it is possible to live, but it's a lot harder."

I don't know what will come of Russia. I don't know whether it can change these habits of passivity, whether it can move past the corruption, whether it can avoid another cycle of authoritarian rule. It is folly to prophesy about a country that has defied our every expectation. The release of Cold War documents by the Central Intelligence Agency confirmed that no one there suspected that the Soviet Union would collapse when it did. The Russians themselves seem lost. Statistics on life expectancy show a distinct rise in despair—men and women have taken to drink, often because they have lost faith. Outside the glittering limits of Moscow and St. Petersburg, life, for most people, has become more difficult. Yet there is a new freedom, and there are the hundreds of thousands of young Russians who have found a place in the new economy, who have discovered the world through travel and the Internet, who no longer feel abashed before foreigners. Though billions of dollars have fled the country, many people believe that a sizable portion would return if the economy stabilized and the government created a rational tax policy. The worst, optimists insist, is over.

I don't know. But I look at the faces in these images, the eyes, and I know that however gray their world, however hard, they will persevere, and will find those moments of peace and beauty that they so richly deserve.

Above all, you have to understand the vastness that was the Soviet Union, and still is Russia. "One-sixth of the earth's surface" beggars comprehension. What best illustrates it was my first flight to Vladivostok, in the Far East. Flying from Moscow took 10 1/2 hours nonstop. A third of the time, we overflew an unbroken, dense forest, the Taiga; nearly the size of the continental United States, its population is estimated at 75,000.

Second, Soviets got their first taste—ever—of democracy in 1990. I try to take the long view and see this particular glass as half full; not a generation has passed since the end of a thousand continuous years of absolute authoritarian rule. It will surely take a full generation's time before Soviets live in sync with the rest of the industrial world.

What name to use for the amalgamation of fifteen now independent countries, which together so closely resembled Catherine the Great's empire, and which changed names during the time covered here? Nearly everyone living there still uses the term *Soyuz,* "the Union," as if the entity had never dissolved. "USSR" is never used these days, and it is impolite and inaccurate to use "Russia" in its stead. For simplicity's sake, at the cost of accuracy, I will mostly use "Soviet Union."

54

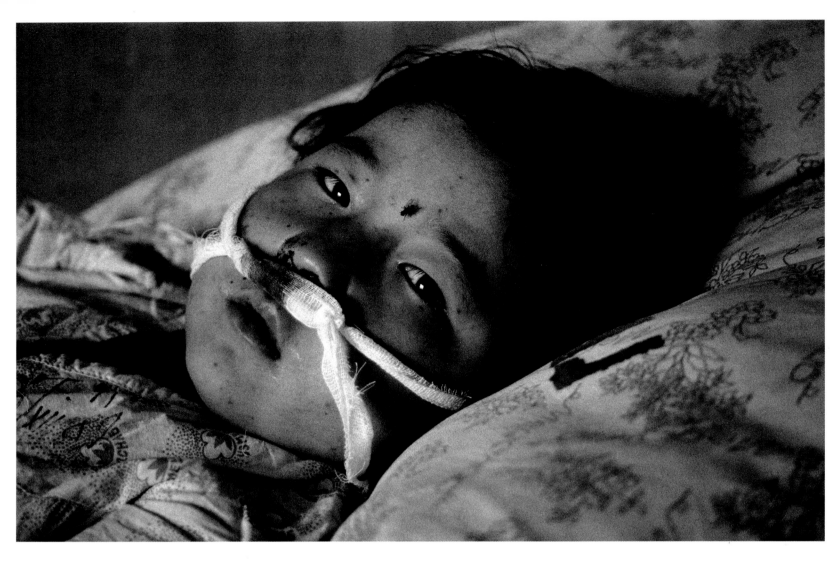
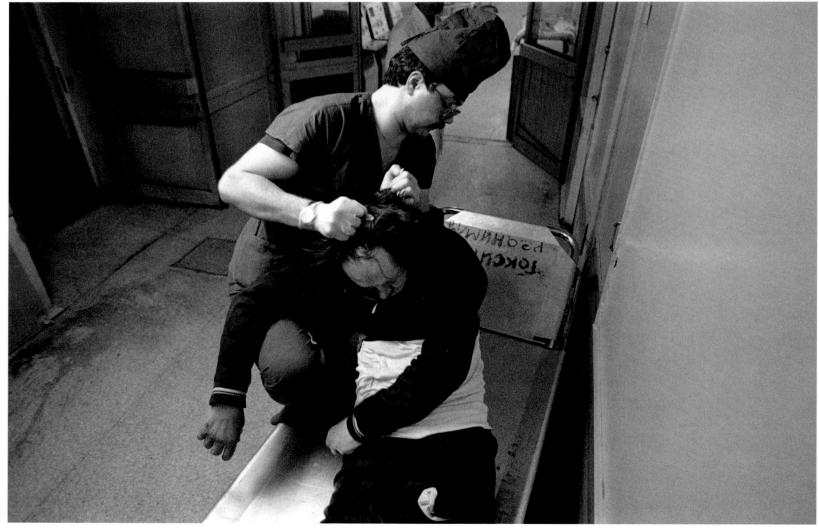

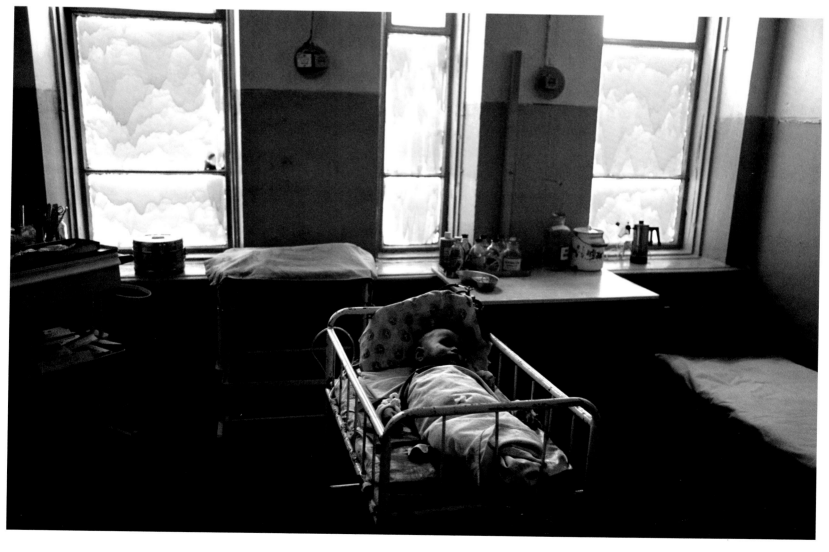

pages 24–25
**OCTOBER 1992** Eight time zones east of Moscow, the Kuril Islands archipelago is in every way an extension of Japan—except in fact. The Soviet Union snatched the island chain as loot following the Great Patriotic War of 1941–45, in which the Soviets declared war on Japan only after the atomic bomb was dropped on Hiroshima. The Soviets resettled the islands exclusively with Slavs to impress the point of a permanent transfer. These islands remain an ever-inflamed issue in Russo-Japanese relations, and the reason (some say the excuse) why Japanese aid to the former Soviet states has been negligible. Natural resources here are few but formidable; salmon and crab are plentiful, and the surrounding sea is a rich fishing ground. There are huge natural harbors. Above all, the Kurils provide a strategic line of defense for the Union's eastern flank. These low, windswept islands bristle with radars, tactical fighters, and anti-submarine bases.

Subject to ferocious typhoons and earthquakes, this is the heart of the Pacific "Ring of Fire." The answer to why anyone would want to live here is contained in the Kurils' very remoteness. Since 1945, everything, including orders from Moscow, takes weeks and months to arrive. There is plenty of fish to eat, and red caviar by the liter. Few visitors of any stripe mean few surprises in a system that fears the unexpected. To say that life here, even military life, is relaxed, is not to make too fine a point. Absent international crisis or natural disaster, people are content to go slowly about the business of everyday life. In the administrative headquarters in Yuzhno Kurilsk, the official visitors' log dates back to the 1960s; I am the eighth Western visitor to register in it. I have traveled to many places in the world but have never felt more remote, more cut off from everywhere else, than in this gloomy, gray place. Strange, considering that Tanfelyevo Island, at the southernmost tip of the Kurils, is only six miles from Hokkaido, the northernmost island of Japan. As a constant reminder of their presence, the Japanese built a huge white tower on the beach, clearly visible across the water.

A perquisite of living in this seismic rollercoaster is an abundance of volcanic hot springs. Traditionally lovers of saunas and mineral baths, Russians, Ukrainians, and Byelorussians cast concrete bathtubs around the islands wherever the opportunity presented itself—in this instance, on a rocky beach near the town of Kurilsk, Iturup Island. The man is a truck driver on his lunch hour, enjoying a hot soak in the cold drizzle. The ship was a Japanese coastal freighter, blown ashore in a typhoon. Its hulk will be left to rust.

pages 26–27
**DECEMBER 1992** Twenty degrees below zero, but the wash still must be done at Severnoya Kirovsky State Farm in Kazakhstan, where it meets Russia, Mongolia, and China.

page 28
**JUNE 1992** A favorite summer vacation spot for Soviet families has long been Sochi on the Black Sea. Sochi is as close as Russia gets to a subtropical climate. Its rest houses and sanatoria used to be filled with the families of favored workers and *apparatchiki,* but these days Sochi has fallen on hard luck. The *nomenklatura,* the big bosses, always hid away in their dachas above the city, and they were always running away to see *their* bosses in the Crimea. But the newly privatized industries no longer reward their workers with vacations here or anywhere else, and the affluent like to go abroad for a rest. (A "rest" is a vacation. A "holiday" is, or used to be, a day of marching or other unpaid political work, and hugely unpopular with everyone except kids. "Holidays," in turn, were not disliked as much as "Black Saturdays"—mandatory, "voluntary" unpaid days at work.) The traveler to Sochi will now find, besides the sun and warm water, a thriving black market in Turkish goods, lots of petty crime, low-rent gambling casinos, and prostitutes everywhere.

page 29
**AUGUST 1993** A lazy weekend in the village of Zagoryansky, twenty miles east of Moscow, on the Klyasma River. This is dacha country, where the Soviet middle class—those with favored jobs or influence—built weekend cottages. Most houses are modest, but the ostentatious villas of the nouveau riche are beginning to sprout here and there.

pages 30–31
**FEBRUARY 1992, Yamal Peninsula, Siberian Arctic** 72.5°N by 70.3°E, −76°F. A family of Nentsy people moving its reindeer herd from the moss-growing tundra at the Arctic Ocean (more graphically in Russian: the Northern Ice Ocean) to slaughter in the Khanty-Nentsy Autonomous Region, 1,200 miles south and four months' travel from here. They will arrive home in June and rest for a month. Then they will begin the journey north again with a new herd; the latest reprise of a thousand-year-old cycle. Pretty much left alone by the state, the Nentsy's concession to seventy-three years of Communist rule was to label each family group a "collective" and sell their reindeer meat only to official buyers. They were free, however, to sell reindeer horn to buyers from China, who prize it, in powdered form, as an aphrodisiac.

page 32
**APRIL 1991, Moscow** Wearing a stylish Astrakhan, or persian lamb, hat. It is considered a sign of status.

page 33
**MAY 1992** A Sunday walk in Osh, Kyrgyzstan's industrial city.

pages 34–35
**APRIL 1991** The good side of Brezhnev's housing policy in the 1970s was that it built millions of units of sorely needed shelter. The bad side was that they were mostly poorly designed, prefabricated concrete "instant slums," built with leaky plumbing, unsafe wiring, few sidewalks or other public amenities, no shops, and, frequently, limited access to transport. These problems had to be addressed after families moved in, often after years on a waiting list. In one such Moscow suburb, I heard these buildings called "sleeping wagons," presumably comparing them to the boxcars-with-benches of old Soviet second-class railway cars. Shown here is coal miners' housing in Novokuznetsk, Kuzbass region, Siberia.

page 36
**APRIL 1991** Novodevichy Cemetery is Moscow's Père Lachaise, the final resting place for VIPs. Gogol, Khrushchev, and Molotov are buried here. Observing an old Russian custom, the family of the deceased designs and builds the tombstone (which the state may or may not pay for) and cares for it in perpetuity. The family of this late general wrapped his tombstone in plastic to protect the fragile marble from air pollution and acid rain.

page 37, *top*
**APRIL 1992, Kadamjai Antimony Complex, Kadamjai, Kyrgyzstan** The true boss of a factory is usually not the director or even the deputy director. It is the local Party chief, who may hold any job in senior management. He (I've never seen a she) determines who is hired and fired, allocates the easier jobs, housing, vacations, access to special shops, and all the factors that make life easier in an industrial community. Some do this job in the background. Some don't care who knows. In the transition from old system to new, the Party boss tends to stay on top.

page 37, *bottom*
**MAY 1991, V-E Day anniversary, Gorky Park, Moscow** Twenty million died in the Soviet Union during the Great Patriotic War.

Like the Civil War in America, it was the watershed event in the country's history. There are relatively few old men to be seen today, so great was the carnage. Survivors, men and women alike, often wear their service bars every time they go out in public. On important occasions, they wear their medals as well, just as many as Civil War veterans did in America.

pages 38–39
**DECEMBER 1991** Dating from the tsar's day, Passage Department Store was St. Petersburg's answer to Moscow's GUM, but more fashionable. That was then. Now, Passage is the epitome of *Sovyetski servis*—Soviet service—a phrase that captures the dark humor of the Soviet people. It means customers are an intrusion on the lives of salespeople, who are unafraid to loudly educate the unaware. Specifically, it illustrates the minor role that consumer goods play in the Soviet scheme of things. It also symbolizes how deeply the ordinary Soviets paid their share for the Cold War. By contrast, Westerners pay high taxes but demand quality and choice in consumer goods.

Since Brezhnev's time, this enormous wedding cake of a store (built around 1900), with thousands of employees, has had essentially nothing to sell that anyone is interested in buying: hazardous appliances, shabby housewares, stodgy, ill-fitting clothes, cheap souvenirs, and badly painted Matrioushka nesting dolls. (The word *brak* in Russian means "junk." When my assistant, Sergei, wanted to know the English word for the dolls and souvenirs on offer here, I called it "bric-a-brac." He found this hilarious.) When anything of value arrives in stock, the employees' friends and families clean off the shelves instantly. From this came the Soviet term "throwing out" goods, as opposed to things being offered for sale. Pity those on a fixed income who have nowhere else to buy a cooking pot or a winter coat.

page 40
**MARCH 1992** Cafeteria, Dyetski Mir (Children's World) Department Store, Moscow. If there was ever a taboo against being drunk in public, it has been irreparably broken.

page 41
**MAY 1992** "Nyet!" A relic of Gorbachev's 1985 alcohol suppression campaign, which lasted somewhere between "He must be crazy" and a year, depending on whom you ask. Official toasts were to be made with fruit juice. Many vodka distilleries were closed down. The art of making *samogon*, moonshine from potatoes, and *barga*, homemade beer from black bread, was revived. Seven years later, only the remotest corners of the Union (such as here at Party headquarters for the Chardjou region, Kara Kum Desert in Turkmenistan) show any traces of the campaign, which, coincidentally, happened at the same time Americans were being exhorted to "Just say no!"—with exactly the same results.

Russia's rulers have bitterly complained about their countrymen's obsession with alcohol almost since the seventeenth century. If a foreign photographer gives a party for colleagues in his Moscow apartment, it can be expected that some of his Russian guests, educated and professional people, will drink until they pass out on the sofa or the vodka runs out, whichever comes first. Awakening in the morning, they make sincere apologies, thank their host, and take their leave. No offense is intended and no hard feelings are expected.

The top on all domestic vodka bottles is a thin aluminum cap with a long tab on its side. Because of the resemblance, everyone calls it a "sailor's cap." Once torn off, it cannot be replaced. The vodka is expected to be drunk until the bottle is empty.

page 42, *top*
**MARCH 1991** A Sunday stroll in Tiraspol, "Transdniester Republic," Moldova.

page 42, *bottom*
**MAY 1992, Osh, Kyrgyzstan** A monument to the first pickup truck made in Kyrgyzstan. Also put on pedestals all over the Soviet Union were tractors, cars, tanks, turbines, hand tools, combine harvesters, and giant lumps of coal. Bill Keller of the *New York Times* once told me he had seen a monument to a refrigerator. I hope in vain that these optimistic, goofy tributes to Progress stay on display forever as objects of art.

page 43, *top*
**JANUARY 1992, Nadim, Tyumen region, Siberia** Orthodox Christmas may be celebrated on Twelfth Night in early January, but the Western custom of Christmas trees is taking hold.

page 43, *bottom*
**MAY 1992** The Dove of Peace is portrayed often in many ways in the Soviet Union, but I don't remember ever seeing one look quite so edible as this one at a bus stop in Kyrgyzstan.

pages 44–45
**MAY 1992** No refrigerator in this eight-family *communalka* in Ashkabad, Turkmenistan. Although the building was badly damaged by the devastating Central Asian earthquake of 1948, it has never been repaired. Like the families with which she shares the building, this woman is an ethnic Russian who has lived in a communalka all her life. (There are 25 million Russians living in the fourteen independent countries that made up the USSR along with Russia.)

In the big cities, a communalka is a large apartment shared by two or more families, with a common kitchen, bathroom, and toilet. A whole building devoted to this purpose, even a small building such as this, is rare. Most often, a whole family shares one room. When Brezhnev came to power, as many as one-third of urban Soviets lived in communalki. This form of housing became the state's politically acceptable way to bridge the problem of chronic shortages. It was also a way to work around the issue of people working without the correct *propiska*, or residency permit. (Westerners call the propiska "the internal passport." I believe Russia will become a truly democratic country only when the propiska is abolished.)

page 46, *top*
**MAY 1992** On the edge of the Kara Kum Desert, Turkmenistan, the ancient Silk Route ruin of Merv lies undisturbed, except for some herds of camels. Widespread interest in Central Asian archaeology has come alive only since the 1980s, when Western academics were permitted to participate.

page 46, *bottom*
**FEBRUARY 1992** In the Bovorenkovo Gas Exploration Camp, Yamal Peninsula, Siberia.

page 47, *top*
**MAY 1992** On the border between Turkmenistan and Iran.

page 47, *bottom*
**MARCH 1992** These days, most collective farms are poorer than usual. To save gasoline, this farm near Rostov-on-Don uses a horse-drawn wagon to haul meat from the abattoir to the collective kitchen. When beef or pork is not available, they will eat horsemeat.

page 48
**MARCH 1992, near Novabad, Tajikistan** Tajiks are the only Soviet people whose language and customs are related to Iran and Afghanistan, though, like all Soviet Central Asians, they read and write using the Cyrillic alphabet. Tajikistan is the most remote republic, and

shares a long border with Afghanistan's mountainous Hindu Kush. The bulk of the country is hidden behind rough mountains and glacier valleys. The combination makes for narrow, free-flowing rivers, which are regularly tapped for hydroelectric power. After cotton from the flatlands and silk from the foothills, hydropower is Tajikistan's biggest export. Five million people live here. Dushanbe, the capital, is home to half a million Russians and as many Tajiks. There are many Uzbeks in the flat farmlands.

If geography is history, it is more true here than most places. The nine-year Soviet invasion of Afghanistan ended in 1989, setting free the genie of nationalism in Tajikistan. On one side is the secular government, supported by Moscow and Dushanbe's Russians; on the other are nationalist religious factions, supported by Afghanistan. Loyalties throughout the country appear to be divided equally. Armed clashes started three years ago and show no sign of abating. Although Russia is terrified of an Islamic phalanx along its southern borders (and a sudden influx of millions of refugees), Tajiks traditionally do not closely identify with their Turkic-speaking Central Asian neighbors.

### page 49, *top*

**APRIL 1991** A village in the Siberian Altai region, populated by Volga Germans and their descendants. Deported from the Volga River valley by Stalin in 1941, these self-sufficient, disciplined people are gradually moving back to the fertile Volga land. Some have taken advantage of the German Law of Return, which guarantees them citizenship, but news of the problematic reception of former East Germans is closing down that avenue. Russia can ill afford to lose these peaceful, efficient farmers.

### page 49, *bottom*

**NOVEMBER 1992** Ground zero—the site of the first Soviet atomic explosion (and continuing explosions until the Test Ban Treaty of 1963). Lt. Col. Alexander M. Krasilniy, atomic safety engineer, Army of Kazakhstan, looked at me for a reaction. We had just walked away from the spot where the Cold War turned deadly earnest. A grassy crater on the plain, no more than ten feet deep and fifty yards across. Here, on August 29, 1949, the USSR detonated its first atomic bomb. Hot spots of radiation remain, so the officer often glances at his Geiger counter. He is my guide to the Kurchatov Atomic Test Range, near Semipalatinsk, Kazakhstan, located in the "Polygon," a vast, closed military area straddling the Russian-Kazakh border. He had asked what I thought about the place. Looking at chunks of vitrified concrete and melted steel girders poking through the soil, I told him this was the saddest place I'd ever seen, instantly regretting my candor. I had broken the rules by not saying simply, "Very interesting."

### pages 50–51

**APRIL 1992** A boy taking a shortcut home from school in Almaty (Alma Ata), Kazakhstan, walking on top of the transport cases that until recently held mobile, nuclear-tipped ballistic missiles. The missiles were destroyed in accordance with the START treaties.

### page 52

**JULY 1993** Asking for directions on a country road in the Ukraine, we get pointed two different ways at once.

### page 53

**MAY 1992** With its harsh winters and enormous size, the Soviet Union was never renowned for the quality of its roads. Even fewer resources are put into highway upkeep in the independence-minded Baltic states. An exception is the road to the airport from Vilnius, the capital of Lithuania. Whether built to impress visitors or for other reasons, it is a modern four-lane, divided, limited-access highway. Locals travel it as often as they can. They call it "Fifteen Minutes in America."

### page 54

**MARCH 1992, near Nurek, Tajikistan** The national sport of Tajikistan is *Buzkashi* (in Russian, *Kozlodran,* or "tear the goat"), which is frenetic polo played by one hundred horsemen at once. A goat carcass is the "ball." Before the advent of the goat carcass early in the twentieth century, the head of an enemy killed in battle was used. Until Gorbachev's time, the game was forbidden by the government, which called it a nationalist throwback. Tajik culture reveres horses. Horsemen all over Tajikistan compete on Sunday afternoons for color TVs and other prizes.

### page 55

**JULY 1991** There are two ways to buy a car in the Soviet Union: from an official waiting list at a state garage, or at the free markets that exist on the outskirts of nearly every Soviet town. The advantage of buying from the state is that a new car costs only $100, about six months' wages. The disadvantage is that you will wait between seven and ten years for your car, if it comes at all. At the free market, such as this one near Sukhumi, Georgia, a nearly new Zhiguli (a 1970s-era Fiat design also known as a Lada) costs about $2,000, or ten years' wages.

### pages 56–57

**APRIL 1992, Dushanbe, Tajikistan** Orthodox Islam is not widely practiced in the republics of Muslim Central Asia, but traditional customs are. Visitors often mistake the latter for the former. An example is the Sunday bazaar, the only place where unmarried boys and girls are permitted to speak to one another in public. Everyone comes here, in his or her best clothes, to buy some pistachios or sell a length of silk, but mostly they come to gossip. The bazaar is a lubricant that reduces friction between those natural antagonists, Sunni Islam and Communism. Party and religious leaders alike listen closely to the hum of the bazaar, for here is where the people's pulse is taken, news is spread, and rumors are started or quashed.

### page 58, *top*

**MAY 1992, Mari, Turkmenistan** In the post office, waiting to make a call.

### page 58, *bottom*

**MARCH 1992** An ordinary winter day, Surgut, Tyumen region, Siberia. The steam is coming from the power plant.

### page 59, *top*

**MARCH 1993, October Square** The biggest statue of Lenin in Moscow.

### page 59, *bottom*

**MARCH 1992** Sunset, Almatyevsk, Tataria.

### pages 60–61

**APRIL 1991** Munyak, Uzbekistan, was a fishing port on the Aral Sea, once the fourth-largest body of fresh water on earth. Stalin wanted a certain supply of gun cotton, so he diverted water from the Syrdaria River in Uzbekistan and the Amudar River in Kazakhstan to irrigate cotton fields. Now the greatly expanded crop goes to foreign textile mills for hard currency. The Aral Sea has shrunk to half its former size and has broken into two bodies of water. The shore is now thirty miles away from Munyak and receding by the month. Without fishing, people here have little to do. They suffer perhaps the poorest health in the Soviet Union: Dust containing pesticide residue from the cotton fields is carried in daily wind storms from the dry lake bed. Anemia is found in 95 percent of the population; throat cancer, astonishingly, kills 5 percent. Nearly everyone suffers some kind of skin disease. Infant mortality is the highest in the Union, and all infants are underweight. Life expectancy has fallen to fifty years, a level characteristic of the third world.

The Republic of Uzbekistan has no interest in helping. The government considers the Karakalpaks who live here a rival tribe who would only revert to their independent fishing and farming ways should the Aral Sea be brought back to health. The neighboring Republic of Kazakhstan, which shares jurisdiction with Uzbekistan over the Aral Sea, considers it an Uzbek problem. So the Karakalpaks of Uzbekistan continue to die off at the highest rate in the industrialized world.

**page 62, top**
**MAY 1992** The children's hospital in Nukus, the capital of the Autonomous Republic of Karakalpakstan in Uzbekistan. Suffering from leukemia, this child needs equipment and medication that the hospital does not have.

**page 62, bottom**
**MARCH 1993, Moscow** The Toxicological Trauma Clinic, at Sklifovskaya Central Hospital, is the emergency destination for alcohol abusers passed out on the street, who may be in danger of alcohol poisoning, hypothermia, and related illnesses. Members of the medical staff here say they must be the most experienced in the world at this kind of treatment. It is a little like an assembly line. Many severe alcoholics are in danger of gastrointestinal bleeding. They are wheeled in, their stomachs are rinsed with a cold water lavage, IVs are inserted, and vital signs are monitored. The patients sleep it off and walk away in the morning. The cycle will repeat itself, doctors tell me, until they die of cardiac arrest or methyl alcohol poisoning.

**page 63, top**
**JUNE 1992, Lake Ysyk-Köl (Issyk-Kul), Kyrgyzstan** Muslim by tradition if not in practice, rural Kyrgyz hold a funeral the day after death. The whole village attends for a prayer, a meal, and a burial. There is a shroud, not a casket. The fog of shock has lifted just enough for this young woman to realize that her mother is no more.

**page 63, bottom**
**APRIL 1991** Fatalities among babies and the very young are so relatively common in Munyak, Karakalpakstan, a room has been set aside in the local hospital to accommodate their families. Here a two-year-old has died of respiratory disease.

**page 64**
*Top:* Rural Moldovan woman; Tatar man; Russian boy
*Middle:* Kyrgyz man; Turkmen woman in traditional dress; Moldovan man
*Bottom:* Armenian Soviet soldier; Uzbek man; Russian woman

**page 65**
**JUNE 1992** Uzbek girl, near Bukhara, Uzbekistan.

**pages 66–67**
**APRIL 1991** A crowd of Moldovans gathers in front of a Soviet Interior Ministry police station in the center of Kishinev, the capital of Moldova. It is Referendum Day in the Soviet Union, and voters are being asked to approve changes to the Constitution. Moldovans want total independence; they are boycotting the referendum. The police station is a polling place. The crowd here is determined to block any Russian-speakers from coming to vote. The Interior Ministry police keep to their barracks.

**page 68**
**OCTOBER 1992, near Yuzhno-Sakhalinsk, Sakhalin Island**
Early in World War II, Japanese soldiers abducted more than 60,000 young Koreans from their homes and shipped them to Sakhalin Island, off Russia's Pacific Coast. There they were forced to work in strenuous jobs, such as coal mining and oil drilling, in the cold, wet climate without warm clothes or proper nutrition. Thousands died under the harsh conditions. The Red Army recaptured the island in 1945. Thirteen years later, all remaining Japanese POWs on Sakhalin were repatriated, but the Koreans and their descendants were not; they were forbidden by Soviet authorities to return to their homeland, even for short visits to relatives. And because there were no diplomatic relations between South Korea and the USSR, South Koreans could not visit their Sakhalin relatives. Soviet-Korean relations, which had never been good, turned poisonous on September 1, 1983, when Korean Airlines flight 007, a Boeing 747 with 269 people aboard, was shot down by Soviet jets when it strayed over the waters near Sakhalin. An agreement was finally reached in 1990 that allowed small groups of surviving victims to visit South Korea for thirty days. Arriving there, they found few living family members, and most of those were poor farmers who could offer only modest financial support. While their educated, bilingual grandchildren hold hope for some kind of future, the 43,000 survivors of kidnapping speak bitterly of abandonment and life in a cul-de-sac of history.

The photograph shows second-generation Sakhalin Korean girls preparing for a traditional dance in honor of village elders. Later in the day, the forty elders will board the first ever Korean Airlines flight from Yuzhno Sakhalinsk to Seoul. Once there, they will spend a month searching for lost relatives, and then return to Sakhalin.

**page 69**
**JULY 1993** A Russian girl in Kishinev, Moldova. Every Sunday from spring through fall, wherever you find Russians, you can see little girls wearing big, brightly colored bows in their hair. It is a very old custom. They wear bows in every color. In a crowd, they look from a distance like a bouquet, or a flock of tropical birds.

Moldova was traditionally part of Romania, their languages nearly identical. It was ceded to the Soviet Union after the Great Patriotic War. Since then the small Slavic minority has grown to more than 25 percent of the population, breeding conflict with the majority. The Slavs are happy to live here: this tiny country (the size of Maryland) has a higher standard of living than Russia, and the climate is mild. Whether they can continue to live here is part of the bigger question of what will happen to the 25 million Russians living in the fourteen former republics of the Soviet Union.

Logic would dictate that those with the most oppressive jobs would be the least supportive of the system. Logic would be wrong. The serf mindset fit perfectly into the thinking of *Homo Sovieticus:* If I work a little bit harder, the quota will be met, and no one will point a finger at me; if I dedicate myself more, ideological disharmony will be overcome. To this might be added the serf's wish: If I keep my head down, it will not be chopped off, and if I don't prosper too much, no one will notice me.

*Bardak* is a very rude Russian word meaning "whorehouse," always spoken in dismay at disorganized shops and offices, chaotic and overcrowded transport, even traffic on bad roads. In the dotage of the Soviet system, bardak became a way of life. At a factory in Öskemen (Ust Kamenogorsk), Kazakhstan, for example, an enormous imported tool-making machine was delivered as ordered. No one ever calculated whether it would fit through the door, which could not be enlarged. The machine didn't fit, and it couldn't be disassembled. When I saw it, it was rusting in the snow.

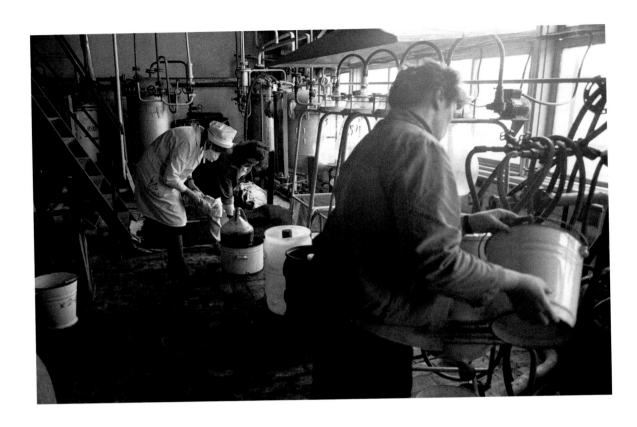

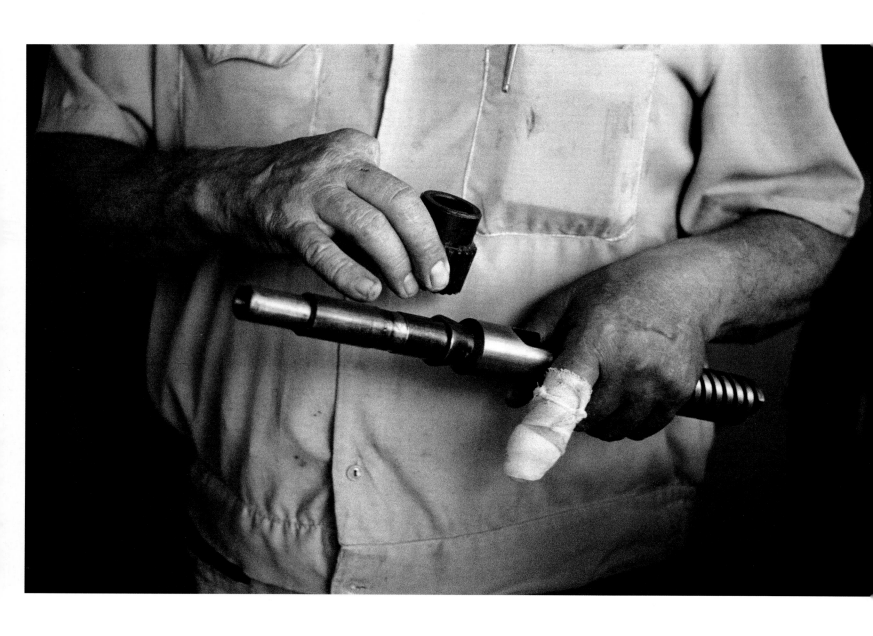

pages 76–77
**NOVEMBER 1991** Raking leaves in front of the Ukrainian State Sugar Beet Company, near Gribionki. The thought is often expressed by rural people: "As long as there is food in the stores, I don't care what happens in Moscow." If Moscow dictates arduous work and political conformity as the price for there being food in the shops, so be it. Moscow's failure to uphold its end of the bargain, above all else, is what brought down Gorbachev.

page 78
**MAY 1992** Installing an irrigation pipeline at the Lenin Collective Farm, near Byshkek (Frunze), Kyrgyzstan. The pipe needs a protective coat of hot tar before it is buried. As with seemingly all Soviet agriculture, men operate machines and women do the heavy lifting.

page 79
**MAY 1992** Alongside fields and market roads, such as here in southern Turkmenistan, near the Iranian border, Socialist Realist statues commemorate the Soviet virtues of Labor, Motherland, and Party. People working near these statues say that, although they resent the Party for its privileged elite and empty promises, they are neither cynical nor bitter about the statues' exhortations. They say they find them inspiring.

pages 80–81
**MAY 1992** Without much machinery, the harvest season means that everyone must be useful, including these children picking cotton on collective farms in the Syrdaria River valley in Uzbekistan.

page 82, *top*
**MAY 1992** The cooking and canning floor, Turkmenrybprom Fish Processing Factory, Krasnavodsk, Turkmenistan. Krasnavodsk is a Russian-speaking enclave on the shore of the Caspian Sea, one of many in Central Asia. The whole town is involved in fishing. This is the town cannery, a state enterprise. All the managers are men, all the working staff women. In May, on the edge of the Turkmen desert, the temperature reaches 90°F daily, with the really hot months still to come. Steam from the pressure cookers reaches everywhere in the plant, and the floors are wet and fish-slippery. It is not the only job available in town and it is not the best paid. I ask them why they work here. They shrug their shoulders.

page 82, *bottom*
**NOVEMBER 1991** As the director of the Ukrainian State Sugar Beet Company walks by with me in tow, the *dezhurnaya* leaps to attention at her post. The omnipresent dezhurnayas are in every factory, office, and hotel in the Union. Their job is to stay in place, watch, be available for action or assistance if need be. There are dezhurnayas whose job is to sit and watch department store escalators. The name is a product of the pre-revolutionary Russian aristocratic classes' infatuation with all things French. Thus, "person on duty" became the *du-jour-naya*.

page 83, *top*
**APRIL 1992** Washing silk cocoons in near-boiling water with no outside ventilation, at the Mrs. Lenin State Silk Factory in Dushanbe, Tajikistan.

page 83, *bottom*
**NOVEMBER 1991** Shoveling corn to feed the swine at the Vni-Imosh State Farm, near Gribionki in the Ukraine. Because winter has begun, so has the task of consolidating the animal feed. The woman facing left is telling the farm director, a man in a dark suit who drives a clean white Volga automobile, to come and pose with them in a photo. He is hiding behind the barn door and won't come out to have his picture taken.

pages 84–85
**DECEMBER 1991** Beryllium and nuclear fuel processing plants, Öskemen (Ust Kamenogorsk), Kazakhstan, site of a disastrous accident in the 1960s that caused thousands of cases of beryllium poisoning. Health scientists rate this the third most polluted city in the Soviet Union.

page 86
**MAY 1992** Sprats are little fish, smaller than sardines, that are served out of the can and are an integral part of *zakuski*, the ubiquitous hors d'oeuvres served to guests in Soviet homes. We are aboard the trawler and refrigerator ship *Krasnavodsky,* flagship of the Turkmen fishing fleet in the Caspian Sea, off the coast of Azerbaijan. The hopper on the right is slowly revolving, filling with live sprats that have been sucked out of the sea by a giant vacuum hose, and then dropped through a chute from the deck above. The conveyor belt moves past, filling empty cans with wiggling sprats resisting their fate. Out of frame left, another man supervises a machine dropping salt, spices, and vegetable oil onto the fish an instant before it seals a lid on the can and cooks it with steam. Meanwhile, our man stands directly over the moving assembly line, intent on seeing the process go smoothly. Amid the din of thumping, clanging machinery, the ash on the cigarette in his mouth gets longer and longer. He takes no notice; he is engrossed with his fish. Bingo! The ash falls, scoring a direct hit into a passing can of sprats.

page 87
**DECEMBER 1991** Kirov Tractor Factory, St. Petersburg (Leningrad).

page 88
**MARCH 1993** Abattoir in the Rumenskoye Agro-Industrial Complex, near Moscow. Although I was permitted to visit many food processing facilities in the provinces and other republics, it took three years to get permission from the Agriculture Ministry to see one in Moscow: a huge new joint venture, a combination abattoir and sausage packing plant, along with a greenhouse and canning factory. Until Rumenskoye opened in 1992, there was nowhere clean or modern enough to show the outside world.

page 89
**MARCH 1993, near Moscow** Black and silver foxes at a fur farm, always a solid generator of foreign currency.

pages 90–91
**APRIL 1992** Smelting pots of antimony, a semi-metallic, blue-white element known for the ease with which it can be alloyed with other metals and for conducting heat and electricity poorly. Antimony is also used in storage batteries, cable sheathing, and paint pigments. It is one of many rare minerals found in the Fergana Valley. Here it is being processed at the Kadamjai Antimony Complex, in Kadamjai, Kyrgyzstan.

page 92
**MAY 1992, Syrdaria River valley, Uzbekistan** Entrance to a cotton *kolkhoz,* or collective farm.

page 93
**JUNE 1991** Every five-year plan had its centerpiece, a new marvel of Soviet ingenuity. Brezhnev's plan for 1971–75 featured the Kama River Truck Factory (Kamaz), which was built in Nabarezhny Chelny (Brezhnev City), Tataria. Within five years of commissioning blueprints, the first truck rolled off the assembly line. Everything needed for the trucks is produced here except glass and rubber. Kamaz is the largest single factory in the world; as late as 1985 it had 160,000 full-time employees. Workers are recruited from all over the country. If that doesn't provide enough labor, soldiers on duty are ordered to work in the factory, as in the case of this young man in the engine shop.

pages 94–95
**DECEMBER 1992** Under the old factory system, it was customary to recognize the most productive or otherwise notable workers by displaying their photos on a very public Board of Honor, such as this one at the Aininsky cotton processing firm in the Dushanbe region of Tajikistan. Only Party members were so honored.

page 96
**DECEMBER 1992** Twenty-five million people worked 50,000 farms in the Soviet Union. Before the 1990s' laws allowing private and leased farming, agriculture was practiced on either *sovkhozy,* state farms, or *kolkhozy,* collective farms. All other farming was technically illegal, but tolerated as necessary to feed the cities. State farms employed salaried workers, had appointed managers, and got first choice of new equipment and fertilizers. Collective farms were—in theory—voluntary associations of individual farmers who pooled their land and resources, elected managers, and divided profits.

At Kaplanbek Sariagash Sovkhoz, in Sariagash, Kazakhstan, the sandy soil and hot summer sun is poor for growing food, but good for growing grapes. Under the old system of controlled prices, the farmers could make a little money if the weather cooperated, and grow enough food to feed themselves and their animals. With prices now decontrolled, they find themselves running a winery that makes theirs one of the most prosperous farms in Kazakhstan. Here, at day's end, vineyard workers wait for their bus home.

page 97
**AUGUST 1993, Bershad, Ukraine** Lunch hour at the Bershad Furniture Factory.

page 98, *top*
**DECEMBER 1991** A frame of pressure gauges at the gas-fired municipal power plant in Surgut, Siberia. Aesthetically, Russians find satisfaction in filling the spaces between phrases in music, thoughts in prose, and lines in art. Even in industry, it is insufficient to leave the instructional function alone; control rooms of nuclear power plants can have a "superfluous" crystal chandelier.

page 98, *bottom*
**MARCH 1993** In the sausage-making plant of the Rumenskoye Agro-Industrial Complex, near Moscow. It's surprising to see so many smiles in this pleasant workplace, the opposite of the usual Soviet work environment. The mystery was cleared up when I asked some workers about their pay. (This is a perfectly polite question in the Soviet Union.) They make a decent salary, but they are also paid in sausages, a much more valuable currency than rubles. These workers know they have something valuable to trade for other scarce commodities.

Before *perestroika,* any worker with access to something of value—a clerk in a store, for example—would alert her network of friends on the arrival of a new shipment of goods. They would come when the stock went on sale (was "thrown out," in the vernacular expression) and buy up (or "take") the goods in the store. Their own needs were satisfied, but more important, they had something to barter, and were now obliged to tell the clerk about anything special that came their way. The system could have kept most of the domestic economy afloat had it not excluded those with nothing to trade: pensioners, most bureaucrats, the lower ranks in the military and police, and, yes, journalists.

page 99
**JUNE 1992** No need to ask what chemicals are made in the Turkmen Agricultural Kombinat, in Mari, Turkmenistan. The piercing smell of ammonia greets a visitor at the front door like a slap in the face.

"Where's the ammonia coming from?" I ask, coughing.

"From the storage tanks," answers the director.

"How long have they been leaking?"

"For years."

I ask to see the ammonia storage tanks. After putting on gas masks, we walk up a flight of metal stairs to a catwalk above the tanks. Our gas masks don't work very well.

"Thanks. Can we go now?" The fumes are worse at the top of the building. Outside, in the air again, I ask the director how long he's been working in the plant.

"Ten years."

Didn't the smell of ammonia bother him?

"You get used to it."

page 100, *top*
**DECEMBER 1992, Chimkent, Kazakhstan** Making a vital heart medication at the Dzerzhinsky Pharmacological Works. This is the only source in the Soviet Union for this medicine. (It's in the bucket on the floor.)

page 100, *bottom*
**DECEMBER 1990** In Borovka, north of the Berezinsky Forest in Belarus, a Soviet soldier works on a hot water tank to be used for the new living quarters of his armored division, which just pulled out of Hungary.

page 101, *top*
**OCTOBER 1992** In the smelter at the Almatinsk Factory for Heavy Machinery, near Almaty, Kazakhstan. Factories are being modernized in inverse proportion to their distance from "the Center," as the government in Moscow is often called. It is a long way from Moscow to Almaty, and the condition of this factory is evidence of that.

page 101, *bottom*
**JUNE 1992, Almalyk, Uzbekistan** Smelting copper and drawing copper cable at the Order of Lenin and Order of the Red Banner Metallurgical Factory, whose name suggests its importance as a source of the red metal. Both factory and copper mine are in the Fergana Valley, the world's richest trove of many strategic minerals. Workers in the valley have always been well paid, so it's no surprise to find support for the old system here.

page 102
**JUNE 1991** Assembling wiring harnesses at the Kamaz Truck Factory, Brezhnev City, Tataria.

page 103
**APRIL 1991** No observer of Soviet industry fails to notice its astonishing waste of resources, labor, and machinery. In the Samotlor oil fields, Siberia, a Japanese-made backhoe is drowned by the side of the road in a pool of spilled crude oil. No one will rescue it.

pages 104–105
**OCTOBER 1992** Making a virtue of necessity: the car wrecks, broken machinery, and industrial detritus of Sakhalin Island finds its way to the Port of Korsakov. It will be loaded onto ships bound for Japan, where it will be recycled in steel mills.

page 106
**MARCH 1992, Rostov-on-Don** The production supervisor at the Rostelmash Combine Harvester Factory is explaining the fine points of machining a steel part, but I can't help wishing he could be a little more careful while working.

page 107
**SEPTEMBER 1991, St. Petersburg (Leningrad)** At the Kirov Machinery Building Factory, the safety officer ordered them to install another fire hose on this floor, so that's what they did.

Faith and belief have always had more profound meaning in Russia and the Soviet Union than in the

West. Spirituality is expressed in ways that Westerners mistake for sentimentality or atavism. We over-

look the Asian philosophical fatalism that pervades Russian and Soviet life, and that this society has

never, to this day, experienced a Reformation or a Renaissance. The choice is conformity or exile, or

worse. That people in such circumstances would be the crucible for a utopian philosophy is not so sur-

prising. The faithful believed in the tsar or Lenin with the same fervency that the Orthodox Christian or

Muslim believes in the deity. In addition, religion itself became a statement of identity, a means of

protest, and even, as the pogroms showed, a deadly weapon.

As Dostoevsky wrote, "If God does not exist, then everything is permitted."

BELIEF

pages 112–113
**MARCH 1991** The Hill of Crosses in Lithuania, a country invaded and occupied so many times over the centuries that its people came to define their nationality by their Roman Catholicism; it alone has remained constant in their lives. It sets them apart in ways that language and social organization do not seem to satisfy. Surrounded by Protestants to the north and Orthodox to the east and southwest, Lithuania shares a small frontier with Poland. But a long history of bloody territorial claims and counterclaims has left no love between the coreligionists. When Lithuania was forcibly annexed by the Soviet Union in 1940, the only (barely) permissible means of expressing nationalism was by the display of religious symbols.

There are different versions of the story of the Hill of Crosses, but this much seems clear: In flat, agricultural north central Lithuania, a small hill, only a hundred yards in diameter and no more than fifty feet high, sits by itself among the grainfields. At its highest point, local people always kept a small crucifix. Sometime after 1940, the authorities had it removed. In the dark of night, another cross would always take its place. This game was played often over the years, but never escalated until *perestroika* time, when several crosses would replace every one removed. Like the brooms of the sorcerer's apprentice, the number of crosses grew geometrically for every one removed. By 1987, thousands of crosses of every kind, big and small, Catholic, Protestant, and Orthodox, covered the hill. When I first visited in March 1991, there were hundreds of thousands of crosses, and a cottage industry had developed nearby, selling more crosses to pilgrims and tourists.

page 114
**DECEMBER 1992** Dawn prayers. A Russian Orthodox nun of the Order of St. Dmitri in the Church of St. Dmitri, part of Moscow Hospital no. 1, built in 1798. In Stalin's time the church was used as a warehouse, but it was otherwise unmolested. (As the compound's buildings are all connected, the preferred method of destroying churches, dynamiting, would have obliterated much of the biggest hospital in Moscow.)

The fifty sisters come from a variety of backgrounds, and they work as unpaid orderlies and nurse's aides in the hospital. The order was founded in 1990.

page 115
**SEPTEMBER 1991** At the Royal Chapel of St. Casimir, patron saint of Lithuania, in Vilnius.

page 116
**JUNE 1992** Tajik boys studying Arabic in their mosque school, near Dushanbe, Tajikistan.

page 117
**JUNE 1992** Street scene in Old Dushanbe, Tajikistan, near the main mosque.

page 118
**MAY 1992** Gravestone in a Soviet Muslim cemetery, near Lake Ysyk-Köl (Issyk-Kul), Kyrgyzstan. In the countryside, cemeteries tell the story of infant and child mortality, which is much higher than in the cities of the European Soviet Union.

page 119
**MAY 1992** Rural cemetery, Tajikistan. The ram's horns, an Islamic symbol for fidelity and strength, are beginning to be seen in cemeteries here, replacing the Soviet custom of Western-style monuments with names, dates, even photos. The conflict in Tajikistan between the religious and secular involves even the dead.

page 120
**JUNE 1992** A family in the courtyard at home, preparing for a Muslim holiday, in Dushanbe, Tajikistan. Following custom, the men have slaughtered a lamb for the evening feast, which will begin after prayers in the mosque.

page 121
**JUNE 1992** Friday prayers in the main mosque, Dushanbe, Tajikistan. Recently expanded, this mosque can accommodate four thousand worshipers.

page 122
**JUNE 1992** An elderly Tajik Koran and Arabic teacher, in Dushanbe, Tajikistan.

page 123
**JANUARY 7, 1992** Orthodox Christmas on Twelfth Night, Moscow. Although New Year's Eve is the most important holiday, Christmas celebrations fulfill the Soviet Union's need this year for continuity with the ancient past, now that history has made a sharp break with the recent past. The young women are in traditional Russian formal dress.

page 124
**FEBRUARY 1991** At the Royal Chapel of St. Casimir, Vilnius, Lithuania. The adults are praying at the catafalque of St. Casimir.

page 125
**JULY 1993** Services in a Romanian Orthodox convent, near Dubossary, Moldova.

page 126
**JULY 1993** Sunday Mass, Romanian Orthodox Church, Dubossary, Moldova.

page 127
**APRIL 1992** The Turkmen wedding ritual symbolically recapitulates ancient tales of bride kidnappings. Here, in Ashkabad, Turkmenistan, the groom's female relatives are leading the bride into the groom's house. They will sequester her and give her gifts until the wedding. Gifts may well include a rug woven by one of the women.

With oval medallions against a deep red field, the "elephant's foot" rug is world renowned, and so closely identified with the Turkmen that it is part of their national flag. (The design is often mistakenly called "Bukhara," after the Uzbek city where it was bought by European traders in the nineteenth century.)

pages 128–129
**JUNE 1992, Ashkabad, Turkmenistan** Turkmen elders leaving the mosque after Friday prayers.

page 130
**JULY 1993** As with Muslim mosques in Central Asia and Baptist churches in Russia, Jewish houses of worship, like this synagogue in Kishinev, Moldova, are seeing young faces for the first time in two generations, thanks in part to the efforts of foreign proselytizing and financial support—in this instance, from the Chabad Lubavitchers. Within the Russian Orthodox Church, these efforts are officially, if tepidly, welcomed.

page 131
**MAY 1991** Delivering flour on a Friday morning to the central synagogue, Tbilisi, Georgia. The flour will be used to bake matzo, the traditional unleavened bread.

**MARCH 1992** Always fearful of being swallowed by their giant neighbor Russia, Ukrainian nationalists nonetheless have never coalesced on what form their opposition will take, religious, political, or economic. With so many Russians living in Kiev and the steppes of the Eastern breadbasket (the borders between the countries are open and unattended), nationwide elections have tended to favor moderates who prefer economic development above all. The second city, Lvov, is a hotbed of anti-Russian feeling (Russians' habit of calling the Ukraine "Little Russia" drives them to distraction), and this issue will take many years to resolve.

At a meeting of officers of the Army of the Ukraine, in Kiev, the organizers are not above using children and religious symbols in pursuit of their cause.

**SEPTEMBER 1992** A wedding party in Yuzhno-Sakhalinsk, Sakhalin Island, Russian Pacific. Everybody's already drunk, including the driver. It is the custom for newlyweds, after a cheerful but subdued ceremony in the Wedding Palace (an otherwise normal government office, but cleaner and freshly painted), to find the highest point in town, survey the panorama, and toast the bride. From here, they drive to the local Great Patriotic War monument, where the bride respectfully lays her bouquet at the Eternal Flame. Then everyone goes to the wedding dinner, at a restaurant if they can afford it, a friend's apartment if they can't. While the whole sequence is fading in Moscow and other big cities, it continues everywhere else, the only variation being that in some cultures they always have the dinner at home.

At the restaurant, there is noisy downing of vodka. Women usually prefer the more genteel *champagnskaya*. Everything is accompanied by *zakuski*, Russian hors d'oeuvres. The band or the DJ plays popular songs, and everyone sings along. The women sing love songs, the men, rousing, up-tempo music—patriotic or army songs if they served in the same unit. Everyone shouts "Bitter! Bitter!" to signify that this is the last time the couple will hear the word—because they will supposedly experience no bitterness from now on. If a stranger is sitting nearby, it's considered rude not to join in the shouts and toasts to the bride. If the stranger isn't sure how drunk or possessive the groom is, it's safer to propose a toast "to the women of Russia!" Or "The Ukraine!" Or wherever one happens to be at the time. The problem with a foreigner chiming in is that, once everyone takes notice, another round of toasts begins. "To the women of America!" Or "New York!" Or wherever the foreigner is from. Before the Party fell from grace, if the couple and their friends or family were Party members, the inevitable toasting "To International Peace And Friendship!" began. We're past the point of being sober enough to order dinner. No matter. The waitstaff serves on autopilot.

Some wedding customs are not dying away, especially those that serve multiple purposes. For example, when a newlywed couple (or anyone else) moves into a new house or apartment, the first living creature to enter the doorway—before any human—must be a cat. It is thought that cats will drive away bad luck in the house. One does not have to keep a cat for this purpose; one borrowed for the occasion will do. Cat owners often provide this service. In the new districts of Moscow in the 1970s and '80s, the need for exorcist cats was so acute that people would often get a kitten for the purpose and turn it loose afterward, never having had any intention to keep it. For years, packs of feral cats stalked the new neighborhoods. It was cruel, but it kept the buildings rat free.

s claimed their prisons were harsh but humane institutions. Most often they were simply ri

e Interior Ministry faced a dilemma: as it struggled to find more public money to improve

ed prisons, it had to deal with more people going to prison for breaking the law in strugg

oney. The problem spiraled downward beginning in the mid-1980s. Overcrowding becam

ally worrisome with the increased transmission of communicable diseases, including HIV.

Under Soviet criminal law, the most common sentence was two to five years. Guns are

y involved in crime, and most violent offenses against people are alcohol-related. Indeed

everyone processed through the criminal justice system is an untreated alcoholic.

Bloody internecine warfare among the Russian mafia makes a good story as it plays out

ies where the international news media live and work. But it does not affect daily life for th

of working poor to the extent sensationalized by foreign observers. It is true that widespre

on in the distribution of food and consumer goods is passed along to consumers as a "mo

More significantly, boardroom and government corruption along with tax evasion hurts ev

in the pocketbook. How President Putin and his successors address this problem will larg

ine the speed with which Russia moves toward "normalcy."

PUNISHMENT

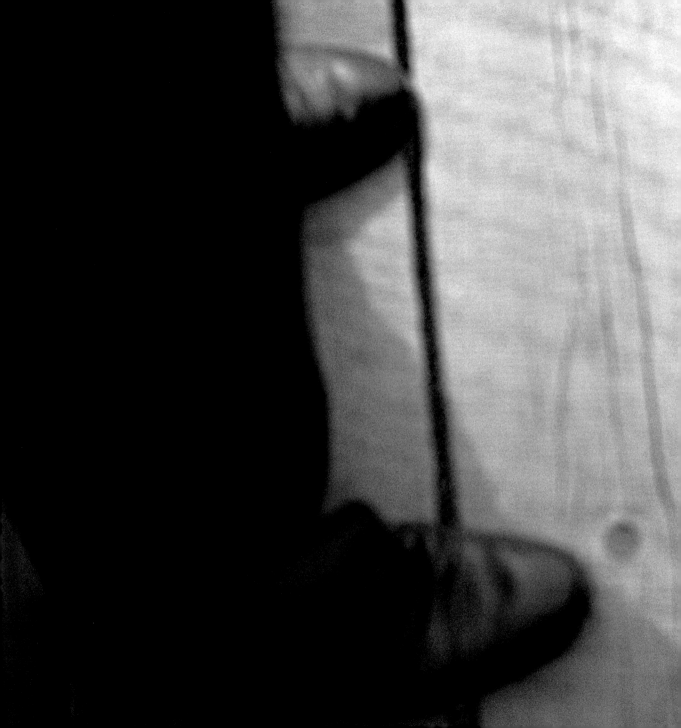

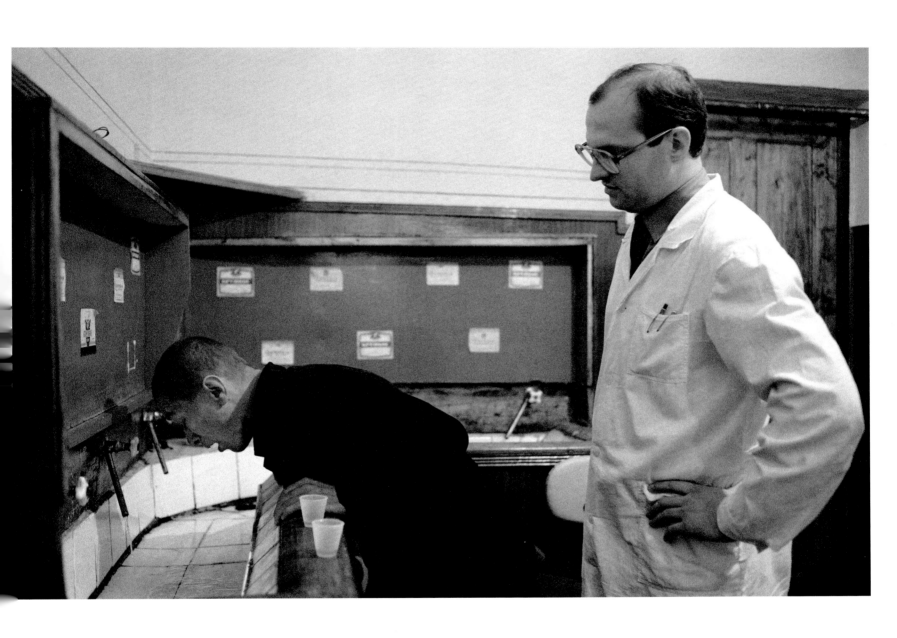

pages 140–141
**JUNE 1991, Yeletz "Harsh Regime—Close Confinement" Prison** There is no life imprisonment under the Soviet system. Short of capital punishment, the maximum sentence is fifteen years. Although there is typically no parole, good behavior, particularly for a first-time offender, often means transfer to a less severe prison. Thus, an inmate may finish his sentence in a different prison than he began it in.

There are five levels of severity, ranging from "Relaxed Regime" to "Harsh Regime—Close Confinement," and variations within those levels. Under the most relaxed, an inmate works all day in the prison factory. At night, he returns to his wife in a nearby apartment provided by the prison. (Exactly the opposite of the Western idea.) For unmarried inmates, administrators will try to find a wife. Most big prisons are in provincial towns, where many men have left to find work in the big cities. Most of the inmates are men from the big cities. Finding a match is not as difficult as it seems: Only a man deemed reformable will be selected, and he is highly motivated to treat his wife gently, considering the alternative. For her part, the woman gets a man compelled to be reliable, forbidden to drink, and whose whereabouts she always knows. Some provincial towns are being repopulated in this way. Prison administrators say this program has been a success, and participation appears to be genuinely voluntary.

At the other end, in "Harsh Regime—Close Confinement," an inmate is never out of a guard's sight. Unruly behavior is constrained by increasing isolation from other inmates. In the tightly social Soviet way of life, physical isolation is agonizing punishment.

The prison in Yeletz, South Russia, is "Harsh Regime—Close Confinement": the most severe in the system. Inmates who are discipline problems at other prisons are sent here, and they usually stay two or three years before being returned to a less strict (and far less costly) institution. They are never allowed out of a guard's sight, and they are searched every time they move from place to place inside the prison. The guard-to-inmate ratio is the highest in the country. Unruly behavior going into or out of the pens is discouraged by an ill-humored, 135-pound German Shepherd police dog. The prison was built in 1835 for its current purpose.

pages 142–143
**FEBRUARY 1992** Fifteen minutes for a silent lunch of soup, black bread, and tea. The fourteen- to eighteen-year-old boys are inmates of the Labor Camp for Boys, in Dimitrovgrad, Ulyanovsk Oblast, east of Moscow in the foothills of the Urals. By law, sentences for youths can be no longer than two years, except for aggravated crime. In that instance, at age eighteen the inmate can be sent to an adult prison, but for no more than two additional years. Sixty percent of the boys here have committed rape, and most of the rest were imprisoned for repeated instances of theft. First-time offending juveniles rarely go to prison. The warden stresses that 40 percent of the boys have no father living at home. He considers this the main factor that led the boys to his institution.

page 144
**JUNE 1991, Yeletz Maximum Security Prison** Inmates are permitted exercise in fresh air one hour a day, pacing back and forth in mesh-roofed pens. They are told not to look up. A sentence in this place can mean not seeing beyond the walls for three years. The *zeks*, or inmates, in this prison are not expected to reform. They are expected to behave according to prison rules.

page 145
**NOVEMBER 1991, Safonovo Strict Regime Prison, near Minsk, Belarus** This is a more typical institution, with dormitory barracks and a prison factory.

page 146, *top*
**FEBRUARY 1992** After lunch in the Labor Camp for Boys in Dimitrovgrad, the inmates gather in the courtyard for a smoke, no matter what the weather. Afterward, they will march in formation to either classrooms or the camp's factory, which assembles handbrake cables for Lada cars. The classroom is considered light duty. The carrot: good performance in class means no work in the factory. The stick: there is a quota of handbrake cables.

page 146, *bottom*
**DECEMBER 1991, Safonovo Strict Regime Prison** "Special Punishment Isolation Cell," the jail within the prison. Thirty days' confinement for fighting, stealing, or possessing a weapon; no bedding, radio, reading matter, or chess set. The window is covered over, and the only way to determine day or night is when the ceiling light is lit or dark. The toilet is a hole in the corner. The cell is warm, but it stinks.

Five prisoners are in a cell with four narrow bunks. The steel tabletop has sharp sides and corners and is too small to sleep on. The floor is too cold, and the walls are too rough to lean against for a prolonged period of time. Therefore, one of them must sleep standing up. The cellmates themselves decide who that will be. That's the "special punishment."

page 147
**FEBRUARY 1992** New inmates at the Labor Camp for Boys, Dimitrovgrad. Boys are unlikely to be imprisoned for a first offense. Second offense or not, these boys just coming into the prison system look dazed and terrified by the experience.

pages 148–149
**FEBRUARY 1992** A classroom at the Labor Camp for Boys, Dimitrovgrad. The classroom was overcrowded and the boys were unprepared for their lesson. I suspect that, in reality, the stick has won out over the carrot.

page 150
**FEBRUARY 1992** After-lunch smoking break at the Labor Camp for Boys, Dimitrovgrad.

page 151
**NOVEMBER 1991, Safonovo Strict Regime Prison, near Minsk** Alcoholic prisoners are medicated with Antabuse, a drug that produces violent nausea when followed by alcohol. The vodka labels on the wall are a Pavlovian touch. The treatment is used on inmates prior to their release. The physician says that more than 80 percent of his inmates are alcoholics.

pages 152–153
**DECEMBER 1992, Labor Camp for Girls, Ligovo Village, Ryazan region, east of Moscow** This is one of two such prisons for girls in Russia. A girl must be convicted of a felony twice to merit incarceration here. Nearly half the girls are serving sentences for aiding their boyfriends in raping another girl. (This proves their devotion to the boy.) Most of the others were convicted of theft, and a few of murder. The sentence for these fourteen- to eighteen-year-old girls is usually two to four years, and only the most severe cases are later transferred to a women's prison. The inmates here were on such good behavior for my visit, so upbeat, it was hard to imagine them ever doing the slightest thing wrong. On other prison visits, I'm ignored by the inmates, or seen as a distraction, a break in the monotony.

page 154
**DECEMBER 1992** Under Soviet law, underage girls are not subject to capital punishment. When I asked the warden at the Labor Camp for Girls

in Ligovo who her most dangerous prisoner was, she took me to meet this seventeen-year-old murderer. The warden said she was more suited to a psychiatric hospital, but they couldn't control her there. She is never permitted out of a guard's sight. There are very few individuals like her.

page 155
**DECEMBER 1992** Interior Ministry Police Colonel Galina Zinovievna Zibulskaya, warden of the Labor Camp for Girls, Ligovo Village, in her office.

pages 156–157
**JUNE 1991, Strict Regime Prison, Öskemen (Ust Kamenogorsk), Kazakhstan** The prison factory. One of the products made here is air cleaners for trucks. Also toaster ovens and other uncomplicated mechanical devices. The *zeks* in this prison are not considered suitable for training. Well-behaved inmates are given time during the day for woodworking shop, where they mostly make elaborate hand-carved chess pieces. Ill-behaved inmates work in the sawmill.

page 158
**FEBRUARY 1992, Labor Camp for Boys, Dimitrovgrad** This inmate works in the prison factory, making handbrake cables for Lada automobiles. A critical Western view holds that Soviet export goods are unsavory and unfair because they are made with prison labor. On the other hand, all heavy industry, including automobile manufacture, is a state enterprise, in which prison labor plays a small role. There are far more soldiers working in heavy industry than there are prisoners. I was never able to locate an entirely prison-made export item, if such a thing exists. Along with the rumors of an American prisoner still held from Vietnam War days, it is one of two futile stories pursued by every new foreign journalist in Moscow.

page 159
**DECEMBER 1992** In the textile factory at the Labor Camp for Girls, Ligovo Village. This shop is an important supplier of firemen's work pants.

page 160
**FEBRUARY 1992** New inmates being processed into the Labor Camp for Boys, Dimitrovgrad.

page 161
**JUNE 1991** Approximately four hundred men and a tiny number of women suffer capital punishment annually in the Soviet Union, a figure constant for ten years (and, it is said, a fraction of the number of secret executions during the Brezhnev years). Executions are for aggravated murder, murder with rape, or serious economic crimes such as embezzling large sums of money from a state enterprise.

This man, a convicted murderer at Yeletz Maximum Security Prison with whom I was not allowed to speak, is awaiting the results of his automatic appeal. It usually takes three months after sentencing to hear an appeal; the trial court's verdict is rarely overturned. For the duration, he is locked in a special cell, where he does assigned work, eats, and sleeps. If his appeal is denied, he must wait until a traveling executioner from the Interior Ministry makes his rounds to the prison. The inmate is taken to a purpose-built room and shot in the back of the head with a single pistol round. His family may then claim the body.

page 162
**DECEMBER 1992** Night rounds in the Labor Camp for Girls, Ligovo Village. The emphasis all day has been on education and rehabilitation, but when the searchlights go on and the facility is locked down, this prison is as coldly secure as any other.

page 163
**JUNE 1991** In the Strict Regime Prison, Öskemen, Kazakhstan.

pages 164–165
**APRIL 1991, Kishinev, Moldova** I have no idea why policemen were chasing this man down the street. They all ran past, and were gone.

The Soviet Union, covering a sixth of the earth's surface, controls the lion's share of the earth's mineral

resources. Soviets take this for granted in the way people on a tropical island are blasé about

coconuts. My editors at *Der Spiegel* report to a country that imports more than a third of its natural

gas from the Soviet Union. They are therefore anxious to know how stable their supplies for electric

power and cooking gas will be. As a result, I (happily) spent a lot of time covering the energy sector

and the extraction of fossil fuels.

ENERGY

Soviets are keenly aware that fuel and raw mineral export is by far their biggest source of

income—the difference between a chance at economic survival and none whatsoever. The ecology

movement, an import from the West, has barely begun to educate ordinary citizens about the conse-

quences of a culture of waste. (Not only in industry: city-dwelling families here produce more waste

per capita than even the United States.) Energy production has been overly labor intensive since the

earliest days. The question, as with so many other industries, is how to become profitably efficient

without pauperizing workers and the surrounding community.

pages 170–171
**MARCH 1991** Main entrance to Raspadskaya Coal Mine, Proko-
pievsk, Kuzbass region, Siberia. The biggest coal mine in Russia, they
say, maybe in the world. (After a while, "biggest in the world" loses all
perspective and meaning here.) The miners are on strike for better
wages and living conditions. Salaries are the equivalent of $50 a
month, not enough to feed their families. Though all are unaware of it
now, the strike is a key factor in the chain of events leading to the
USSR's implosion nine months later.

page 172
**MARCH 1991** Drilling Rig no. 21296, Kaleykemo, Tataria. Having
struck oil a mile below the surface, the drillers are now setting a pipe in
place to start drawing oil from the well. The Autonomous Republic of
Tataria would be world-class rich from its oil wealth, but it is landlocked,
completely surrounded by the Russian republic, and must sell to the
Soviet oil companies at their prices. Complicating matters, Tatars are
Muslims, surrounded by a sea of Orthodox Christians.

page 173
**MAY 1992** Drilling for natural gas, Kara Kum Desert, Turkmenistan.
In a world increasingly divided on the basis of who controls mineral
resources, the Turkmen are betting that they will be winners in the lottery.

page 174
**FEBRUARY 1992** Russian society has always been tightly socialized;
the individual is subordinate to and depends on the group for suste-
nance. What Americans call "personal space" is by and large not recognized here. In Russia, this reflects an uninterrupted millennium of serf-
dom and was a critical factor in the socialist experiment taking hold,
much to the surprise of early Western European socialists. The worst
emotional affliction a Russian can suffer is isolation and ostracism by
the group. Over time, this tight social orientation spread throughout
the Russian Empire and its successor, the Soviet Union.

The exceptions are interesting. In many nations, nonconformists have
always turned to the sea for escape and exile. Without a warm-water
port of their own until the eighteenth century, Russians never related to
blue-water ocean. It wasn't necessary; they had an ocean of trees, the
Taiga. After the Great Schism of 1652–58 in the Russian Orthodox
Church, thousands of the losers of the argument, the "Old Believers,"
exiled themselves to the vast forest thousands of miles to the east. (Old
Believers remain there to this day, aloof from politics.) Following them
over the centuries, whether for political, social, or religious reasons,
many people compelled to leave the group settled in Siberia. The gene-
sis of Siberia as a place of exile was in fact initially self-imposed. It was
later, under the tsar's courts and then the Communists, that imprisonment and brutality became synonymous with Siberia. In reality, Siberia is a
place of vast scope and heartbreaking beauty, with harsh, long winters
of overpowering silence, punctuated by brief, intense summers frantic
with insect and plant life.

This man is a Ukrainian, trained as a mechanical engineer. Some
years earlier, he and his wife came to the conclusion that they couldn't
live under the pressure to conform to life in the Soviet Ukraine. Their
temperaments are milder than those of protesters or resisters, so they
took the socially acceptable if rarely used avenue of applying for work
in a remote part of Siberia. His training made it possible for him to take
a job maintaining a twenty-five-mile stretch of telephone and telegraph
wires at the edge of the treeline in the northern Tyumen region, nearly a
hundred miles from the nearest settlement. Those neighbors are involved
in finding and producing gas and oil. The lines were originally built to
connect an archipelago of nearby gulags that were abandoned in the
1950s but remain largely intact. A one-hour helicopter flight from
Nadim, he lives with his wife in a big, comfortable cottage made of

logs, with eight big dogs to protect them from wild animals, and ample
time to hunt and fish. His work provides a snowmobile and a one-month
summer vacation. He was my guide to the gulag. While we were gone,
the helicopter crew filled the aircraft with fish he had caught and frozen
solid.

There wasn't much chance to speak with his wife; she had just dyed
her hair the day before we came, and it had unexpectedly turned bright
purple. She was too embarrassed to greet her impromptu visitors. Other
than that, they both seem happy.

page 175
**FEBRUARY 1992, near Donetsk, Donbass region, the
Ukraine** In the lamphouse following his shift in the Gorky Coal Mine,
happy as all underground miners everywhere are to be "on the surface"
again. He wants to know how coal miners in America live and how
much money they make. He wants to practice his English with me, and
starts by singing the Beatles' "Back in the USSR," which every Soviet
under age fifty seems to know at least in part, but he can't finish for
both of us laughing.

page 176, *top*
**DECEMBER 1992** One hundred feet below the desert floor, under the
"closed atomic city" of Kurchatov, near Semipalatinsk, Kazakhstan, is
Dr. Alexander N. Kolbaenkov, chief of construction, Atomic Powered
Engine Project for a rocket to Mars. Asked why he would show me this
secret project, Dr. Kolbaenkov offered that the government has run out
of money for the effort, and perhaps the Germans would be interested
in cooperating in the venture? As I represent German media, perhaps I
could spread the word?

page 176, *bottom*
**MARCH 1992** One and a half miles underground at the Gorky Mine.
This is a "low roof" mine: the coal ceiling where miners work most of the
day is approximately four feet above the floor. Most of the time the miners work on their knees. The only way to walk is crouched over a stick,
duck-walking like Groucho Marx in an old movie. It is too strenuous and
time consuming to leave for lunch or trips to the toilet, so miners stay
more or less in place all day.

page 177, *top*
**FEBRUARY 1992** At the Bovorenkovo Gas Exploration Camp, Yamal
Peninsula, Soviet Arctic, once a day someone must look beneath a drilling
rig to see that nothing has come loose, or ice hasn't formed to hinder
some moving part. It is dirty under there, with residue dripping from the
drilling floor above; and it is unprotected and −60°F, with the wind chill
driving it to −100°F. This man completes his survey very quickly.

page 177, *bottom*
**MARCH 1991** During the Kuzbass miners' strike, a supervisor makes
a safety inspection of the mine face and "continuous miner" machine at
the Bolshevik Coal Mine, Abashevo, near Novokuznetsk (Stalinsk),
Siberia.

page 178
**FEBRUARY 1992** Maintenance workers taking a break inside a covered shed at the Bovorenkovo Gas Exploration Camp. Everything here is
under cover from early September until early May. The pace of life here
seems slow and relaxed, but it is really the reaction to three months' of
near constant darkness.

page 179
**APRIL 1991** Roughneck holding a drilling bit, at the Samotlor oil
fields, Siberia. This is one of three oil fields in the Soviet Union that have

produced since the 1920s. The others are Sakhalin in the Pacific and Baku on the Azerbaijani coast of the Caspian Sea.

pages 180–181
**FEBRUARY 1992** At 2 P.M. in early February, it's already dark outside. A weak orange sun rose after ten this morning, loitered on the horizon, and gave up. Sergei, my assistant and a Muscovite, is not used to the intense −50°F cold, so we hurry to the cozy, overheated workers' barracks in the Bovorenkovo Gas Exploration Camp. Another reason he says he doesn't like this place is that it's hundreds of miles past the treeline, and like most Russians he's uncomfortable without trees nearby. (Poems and fairy tales in Russia talk about the enchantment of the forest, just as Western children are raised on tales about the mysteries of the sea.)

All buildings this far north in the tundra sit on pontoons. If builders anchored them on foundations, they would sink into the permafrost during the brief, slushy Arctic summer. This building was home for a week. As a going-away present, the workers gave me the framed portrait of Gorbachev that hung on the wall of their library, which I had once admired in passing. They were as happy to get rid of it as I was to have it. Soviets appear to accept with good humor that Americans love "Gorby," even as they bitterly blame him as the overachieving but impractical "Joe College" who brought on hard times.

page 182
**FEBRUARY 1992** Housing for married workers, Bovorenkovo Gas Exploration Camp. Originally industrial gas tanks, these "barrel houses" are strong, well-lit, insulated, and quite cozy. The weather makes it too harsh for children to live in Bovorenkovo.

page 183
**APRIL 1991** The same industrial gas tank is not considered comfortable housing in Nizhnevartovsk, Kuzbass region, Siberia; there is such an acute and prolonged shortage of housing for oil workers that any shelter must make do. In addition, the ground in subarctic Siberia turns to deep mud in the spring, and there are floods, which combine to make building one's own cottage a futile proposition.

page 184
**FEBRUARY 1992** A coal miner from the Gorky Mine, showered and dressed after work and wearing the emblematic cloth cap of the Donbass region of the Ukraine.

page 185, *top*
**FEBRUARY 1992** Sergei and the camp director walking to the helicopter with my going-away present from workers at the Bovorenkovo Gas Exploration Camp: a portrait of Mikhail S. Gorbachev.

page 185, *bottom*
**FEBRUARY 1992** Yamal Peninsula and the Tyumen fields supply half the natural gas for Western Europe, and a third of the Soviet Union's hard-currency exports. These "Christmas trees" (an oilman's term used everywhere for completed, capped-off wellheads) are not yet tied to the pipeline. With wind chill bringing the temperature to −100°F, connection must wait until spring. By then, handling lengths of steel pipe will not shatter them like glass. The man is the Bovorenkovo Gas Exploration Camp's chief engineer, and we are walking quickly from one drilling rig to another.

pages 186–187
**SEPTEMBER 1992** The Sakhalin Island oil field, Okha. "Okha!" means "Eureka!" Oil has been pumped out of this field since the 1920s, and the landscape shows it. It is estimated that Sakhalin's onshore oil will run out in less than twenty years; offshore exploration and drilling

are now taking place with the cooperation of American and Canadian companies. Environmental groups in Moscow say it may take hundreds of years for the region to recover from the damage of eighty years of oil production. People living in the region have shown symptoms of environmentally caused diseases for years.

page 188, *top*
**FEBRUARY 1992** Street scene in Nadim, Tyumen region, Siberian Arctic.

page 188, *bottom*
**FEBRUARY 1992** Housing in Nadim. These "sleeping wagons" are like all the others from the Pacific to East Germany, but with bigger apartments and better construction to withstand the Arctic winters.

page 189, *top*
**FEBRUARY 1992** Driving in Nadim. A private car is a luxury here, not because the workers couldn't afford it, but because of the month's drive to get the car to Nadim. Goods travel slowly by road and river, and people fly.

page 189, *bottom*
**FEBRUARY 1992** Near the Bovorenkovo Gas Exploration Camp. One reason people do not drive here is that from September to May, there is no way to follow the road beneath the snow unless there are telephone poles alongside.

pages 190–191
**FEBRUARY 1992, Donbass region, the Ukraine** At the end of an eight-hour shift underground in the Zhdanovskaya Coal Mine, half the time spent crawling on their hands and knees in coal dust, for the equivalent of $30 a month. The miners are smoking the second half of the cigarettes they lit this morning, then pinched out to save for this moment.

After photographing coal miners in half a dozen countries, this is what I've learned: In normal times, the money is good, and in bad times, miners have one another to depend on. Miners must work hard and sober, or else imperil their friends, so they attract women who are looking for hard-working men of regular habits. I know of no other compensation for being a coal miner.

page 192
**FEBRUARY 1992** Wire and metal cables are always moving around drilling rigs in the Bovorenkovo Gas Exploration Camp. Drifts of snow bury the frozen cables, which are used for hoisting drilling pipe and other supplies to the drilling platform. Any eight-wheel-drive vehicles that run over them would snap the brittle cables like twigs. The only way to rearrange them is to fish them out of the snow by hand.

page 193
**FEBRUARY 1992** Nadim is a postwar city of 50,000 in the heart of the Tyumen gas and oil fields, above the Arctic Circle. The sky in February is dim, the same shade of white as the landscape. It is sparse, angular, and nearly treeless, with the pervasive silence of all snowy places. The air smells of ice.

Siberians, whether transplanted or native, have always been known as the warmest and friendliest of Soviets. My guide in the gas and oil fields is Valodia, a native Siberian and executive with Tyumengazyneft, the region's oil company and the richest company in the Soviet Union.

After dinner, I retire to a company guesthouse room to write captions and prepare for bed. I have to get a camera to show you why I'm brushing my teeth with vodka tonight. Drilling near the town has let oil infiltrate the water table.

Lenin Steel Mill, Magnitogorsk—formally known as the V. I. Lenin Order of the Red Star and Order of Labor Metallurgical Enterprise, which gives an indication of this factory's importance in the Soviet scheme of things. Popularly known as Magnitka, it was built on a hill of iron ore in the Ural Mountains, eight hundred miles east of Moscow, designed to be safe from enemy attack and prying eyes. This was the centerpiece of Stalin's first five-year plan, 1930–34, conceived to prove that the Soviet state could produce as much steel as the West. ("Stalin," after all, means "man of steel.") The plant was built from scratch in only four years with conscripted labor and sympathetic Western volunteers, and it covers more than twenty square miles. Magnitka made steel for the tanks and guns of the Great Patriotic War, and it continues to do so for cars, trucks, and bridges today. At its peak, it employed more than 100,000 workers and fed half a million dependents. It is a central planner's fantasy and an industrial colossus. It is also a first-rate ecological disaster. But it is too important to the Ural region and the Russian economy to allow it to die.

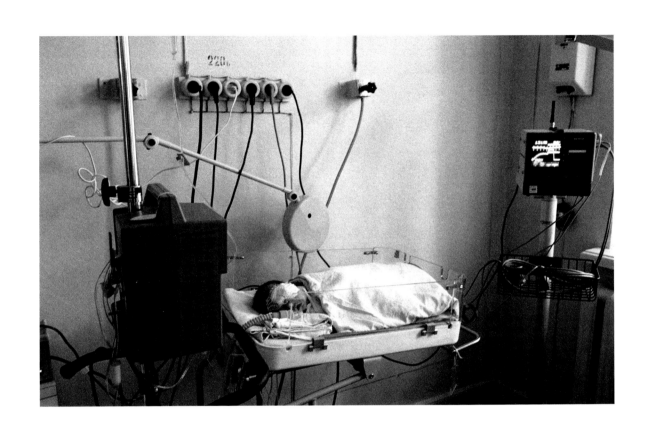

216

pages 198–199
**OCTOBER 1991, Magnitogorsk** A battery of coke ovens. Coke is bituminous coal cooked in an airless oven for about fifteen hours. The carbon-rich residue is mixed in a furnace with iron ore to make iron, the basis of all steelmaking. Other metals and scrap are then cooked with the iron to make alloys with different properties; other-metal content of less than 8 percent makes "low-alloy" steel, and more than 8 percent makes "high-alloy" steels. All steelmaking is some variation of this process.

page 200
**DECEMBER 1991** Smokestacks of the mill from my window at the Hotel Asia. This mill puts black bread on the table for half a million people. It is also arguably the single biggest air polluter in the Soviet Union. It will take billions of rubles to bring the mill to modern emissions standards, and billions of rubles to convert the mill to efficient production methods. At the same time, the mill is struggling to meet its payroll every month. Is anyone interested in buying a very large steel mill?

page 201
**DECEMBER 1991** A blast-furnace worker. He has to walk on hot slag, a sandy by-product of coke, in order to keep the molten iron moving in streams down to the molds. Fifteen minutes on, fifteen minutes off. The fifteen minutes off are not enough.

pages 202–203
**AUGUST 1993** Scenes from the "New Town," Magnitogorsk. Construction of the steel mill was too important to be sidetracked by building housing and shops. From 1930 to 1934, construction workers lived in tents and jerry-built wooden houses, a remarkable sacrifice, considering the Ural winter. By the time the steelmakers began working, construction was under way for brick apartment buildings. Everything was complete by 1939, except no one had planned for expansion. The Great Patriotic War forced such a need. The mill was the forge for the Soviet Union's war industry, and its distance from the fighting turned it into a haven for relatives from danger zones who came to stay with steelworkers' families. Magnitogorsk became painfully overcrowded.

Rebuilding a ravaged European Soviet Union was the priority after the war. It wasn't until the 1970s that Magnitogorsk began to build new housing. The result was the same dreary prefab concrete boxes that marred every other city. Even today, there are many unpaved roads and few shops, and the same weary resignation palpable in the atmosphere of every New Town in the Soviet Union.

page 204, *left*
**OCTOBER 1991** Steel ingots grinding slowly past a mill of furnaces on their way to the hot rolling mill. They are conveyed by overhead cranes and subway-car-sized "mules," or electric locomotives on narrow gauge tracks. The straining of cables, whining of electric motors, and scraping of metal on metal make sounds reminiscent of barnyard animals.

page 204, *right*
**AUGUST 1993** In 1930, a young Margaret Bourke-White, on leave from *Fortune* magazine, photographed construction of the Komsomolskaya (Young Communist) Blast Furnace in Magnitogorsk. The symbolic heart of the steel mill, the furnace was built with the aid of an international brigade of idealists, including Americans. When the mill was completed in 1934, most of the brigadists went home. Some, including a few Americans, fell in love and married local Soviet girls. As their wives were refused permission to emigrate, most elected to stay and put down roots in the Urals. History then conspired to keep these couples from ever leaving. By 1936, Soviet life was crippled by paranoia, show trials, exile, and death by disappearance. The war followed; then suspicion and

paranoia disfigured American public life as well. It was not until the 1980s that these idealistic, elderly men and women were granted exit visas to come to the United States. Most finished their lives peacefully there.

At about the same time, the Komsomolskaya Furnace, already obsolete and having outlived its usefulness, was unceremoniously demolished in 1993. I happened on it by the purest chance.

page 205
**DECEMBER 1991** Molten iron streaming from the bottom of a blast furnace. At this point the iron is 2,200°F. Steelworkers must direct the molten stream through troughs in slag and through steel gates into receptacles called pigs. Working next to flowing molten metal can be dangerous and is always debilitating. This man's job is to ensure the iron is filling the pigs, then to get away as quickly as he can.

page 206
**DECEMBER 1991** This man is not so lucky. He must operate practically underneath a working furnace as it heats the next run. He shovels away excess slag and other residue so that the molten iron flows freely. Other workers wear heavy woolen tunics and pants to keep sparks, drops of iron, and hot cinders off them. Here, it is too hot to wear even that. He shovels a minute, rests a minute, until fifteen minutes have passed, when he can get away and drink cool water and breathe cooler air.

page 207
**OCTOBER 1992** Sweepers below the coke oven batteries. The man on the left is wearing an Astrakhan cap, signifying that he is from the Volga River region of the Caspian. There were no people here before 1930, so Magnitogorsk is a cross-section of every Soviet nationality.

page 208
**DECEMBER 1991** In the "blooming mill," a precursor to the hot rolling mill. Here low-alloy steel is turned into sheets and rolls for making car and truck bodies, refrigerators, and other appliances. Other parts of the mill turn this kind of steel into bars and tubes for industrial use.

page 209
**DECEMBER 1991** Avant-garde of the whole steel mill, and its pride: a modern German electric-arc furnace built in the 1980s. When visitors ask how the steel mill will survive and cope with modern production needs, this is the first place they are brought. Scrap steel is melted down in the vessel, a process by which high-alloy steels can be made. It is a much cheaper and more efficient way of making steel than previous methods used here.

pages 210–211
**OCTOBER 1991** A "furnace room," built in 1934. Nearly a quarter mile long and twenty stories high, it is lined with rows of open-hearth furnaces: the spark-spitting nineteenth-century infernos that enabled the modern industrial world of engineered construction to come into being. It is these furnaces that supply most of the low-carbon steel used in beams for buildings and bridges.

page 212
**OCTOBER 1991** This man's job is to rustproof the steel supports underneath conveyor belts that carry iron ore and ash from one mill to the next. There are miles of elevated conveyors, so the job is never completed. Aluminized paint is applied by spraying it through a hose at high pressure. Over the years, the metal particles have worked their way into his pores and his blood. I am embarrassed to inquire about his health, so I ask how he likes his job. He says he likes to work outdoors. Soviets frequently look ten years older than their age. They often say that visiting Westerners look ten years younger than their age. This man is younger than forty, though he looks sixty.

page 213
**AUGUST 1993** Shooting pictures as if I didn't have a care in the world, with a skilled Russian assistant at my side and American dollars and a Ministry of Foreign Affairs press pass in my pocket, it's easy to forget that, to a Soviet of a certain age, having a stranger point a camera at him on the street means nothing good. It could even have initiated, within living memory, a process ending with a death sentence. My deepest apologies, sir.

pages 214–215
**AUGUST 1993** In the Magnitogorsk Hospital. The twelve-year-old boy *(at left)* developed a painful bone cancer that precludes his sleeping in a bed. Sleeping sitting up, leaning on pillows, is not very comfortable, so he naps intermittently throughout the day and night. His mother spends her days with him, catching sleep when she can.

The pediatrics ward *(right)* has enough neonatal respirators to serve a city of 2 million. Magnitogorsk's population is 500,000. Steel mill smokestacks generate enough air pollution to cause chronic respiratory problems for newborns and their mothers. The ward is always busy.

The geriatrics ward, on the other hand, is not so big or busy; with life expectancy less than fifty-five years for men, most will probably not survive to experience prolonged chronic illnesses.

Sad to say, Magnitogorsk is not a very pretty city. Despite its location in the forested Ural Mountains, only a few species of trees and shrubs survive the dunning air pollution. This is not to say the town is denuded of greenery, but that the variety is very limited. The limited plant life gives the city a worn-out appearance. It also seems that there are fewer people on the streets than otherwise might be, except before and after shift changes at the mill. Smog alerts in winter keep many people inside, and in summer mill workers' families go to special nature retreats in the Urals, nicknamed "oxygen farms." Factory physicians will often prescribe such a rest for workers with respiratory problems. Discussing these problems with people in Magnitogorsk, they often say their problems are nothing compared to those of their neighbor Ural city, Chelyabinsk, which must contend with cleaning up the radioactive pollution from its defense factories.

page 216
**AUGUST 1993** In the Old Town, Magnitogorsk, built 1934–39. The town, replete with housing, shops, cinemas, and parks, was constructed only after the mill was completed in 1934.

There is very little for a pensioner to do in Magnitogorsk, and relatively few survive long enough to collect their pensions over a prolonged time. And as with everywhere else in the Union, there are few old men; so many young men died in the Great Patriotic War. The building here is the Peace Cinema. The letters at the top of the building read, "Forward to the Victory of Communism."

page 217
**DECEMBER 1991** Main entrance to the mill complex. It is also here that pensioners come to collect their checks.

pages 218–219
**AUGUST 1993** Most people all across the country plant potatoes or vegetables in any space they can find. This has been their insurance policy, a hedge against hunger, for the past thousand years. Inflation last year reached 4,000 percent, and there was little food to be found in the state shops. This year it is better, but not much, and food is becoming expensive. Even the families of steelworkers, the industrial vanguard of the state, need a little extra to get by. Their paychecks may or may not come at the end of the month.

pages 220–221
**AUGUST 1993** The coke oven batteries. Someone must work on top of the coke oven to make sure the vents remain clear, and to seal the ovens in order to keep air from getting in. The problem is to stay on top of the ovens long enough to do the job without being burned; the ovens are not sufficiently insulated, and it is uncomfortably hot up here. This man is wearing extra-thick-soled leather boots, and works for fifteen minutes on top of the oven, then cools off away from it for a short while before going back. In the few minutes it took to make these pictures, the bottoms of my sneakers melted. I left part of them stuck to the pavement, like chewing-gum footprints.

page 222
**DECEMBER 1991** Awards given by the Party or factory management for quotas met or exceeded by the hot rolling mill. A retired technician here told me that all the exceeded quotas since 1935 were fictitious. Only the local Cheka (forerunner of the KGB) knew the true figures, and that was the ultimate closely held information.

page 223
**AUGUST 1993** Looking toward the mill from Old Town. At the end of the street is the Gostinitsa Asia, or Hotel Asia, for not-very-important visitors, where I stayed on my first visit. The view from the windows in the rear rooms is unique. The sound and the smell are unique, as well, when the blast furnace is working. The hotel is named after the continent on which it and the mill sit. On the other bank of the Ural River, the town of Magnitogorsk is in Europe.

pages 224–225
**AUGUST 1993** The blast furnace workers on their break. They lack the strength to leave the furnace room and go outdoors, even though it is an August afternoon, and the last breath of summer is still in the air.

The year 1991 began with fearful apprehension in the Soviet Union. Everyone knew there would be

changes. What would they bring? Would there be violence? For many people, food supply was

becoming problematic. Gorbachev's tack to the right in late 1990 led to killings in Lithuania and

Latvia. Western governments clucked in distress but were clueless, as recent disclosures confirm.

The Soviet Union always boasted of its 150 nationalities. Unsaid was whether those nationali-

ties were comfortable with the arrangement, or with one another. Ethnic conflicts, suppressed since

1918, sprung up all over the Union: Chechens fighting Russians; Ossetian Russians fighting Geor-

gians; Georgians themselves in a three-way civil war; Slavs in a standoff with Moldovans; western

Ukrainians eyeing eastern Ukraine; Tajiks in a religious war; Balts agitating for total independence;

and the bloody skirmishes between Armenians and Azerbaijanis over Karabakh. Few in the West

understand the problems of the woeful ecology, a chaotic tax system coupled with institutional corrup-

tion, and the 25 million Russians living in the fourteen nationalistic former republics, ominously called

"the near abroad."

The story of the end of the USSR is not that it ended so badly, but that its people began so

determinedly, in fits and starts, to build their lives anew.

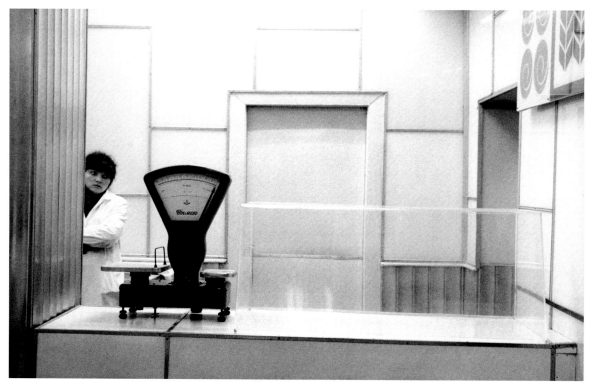

ИЗГОТОВЛЕНИЕ КЛЮЧЕЙ
ИЗГОТОВЛЕНИЕ
КЛЮЧЕЙ
УСТАНОВКА
КНОПОК
УСТАНОВКА
РУЧЕК НА
СУМКИ

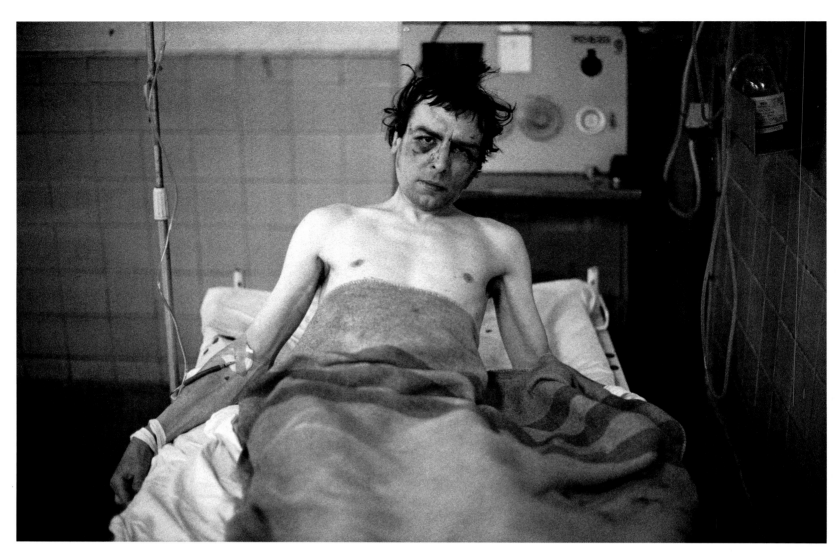

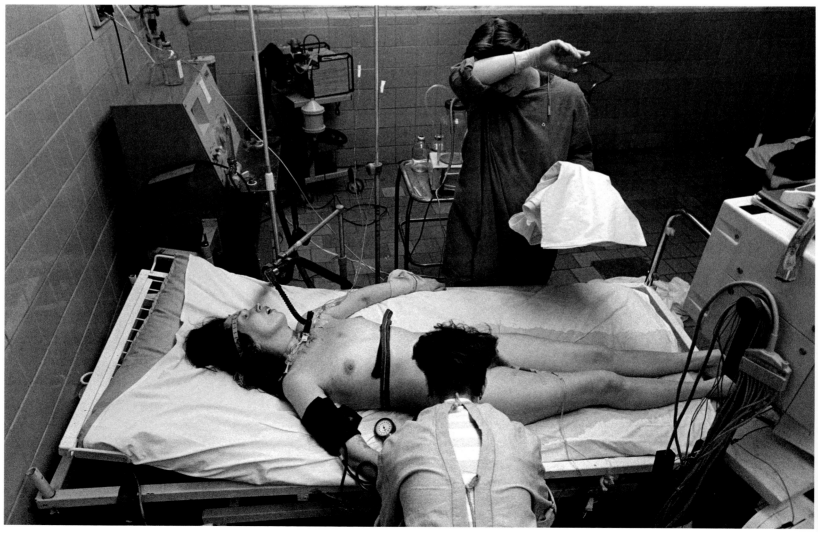

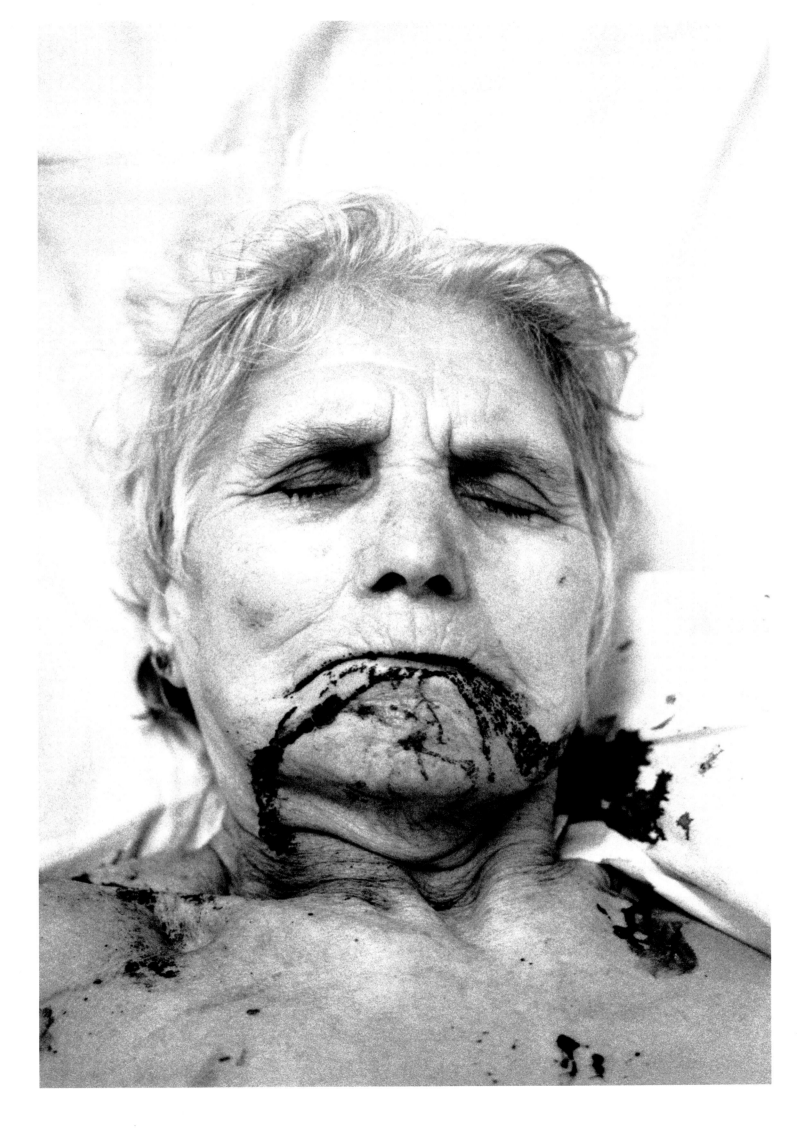

**pages 230–231**

**FEBRUARY 1991, Tallinn, Estonia** For those with hard currency or lots of rubles, delicacies like fresh meat and vegetables are freely available. Since Brezhnev's time, items in short supply in state stores have been known as "deficit" goods. Early on, the term referred to electronic calculators, phonograph records of Western pop music, and the famous shortage of blue jeans. Now, it can mean almost anything—even food is beginning to fall into the "deficit" category.

**page 232, top**

**MARCH 1992** Sever ("North"), a kitchenware shop in Surgut, Siberia. They also sell bathroom sinks without faucets.

**page 232, bottom**

**NOVEMBER 1991, Food Store no. 4, Zaretchny district, Ekaterinburg (Sverdlovsk)** No bread today. Try tomorrow. I am not to blame.

Even the notoriously surly shop clerks can dish out only so much abuse, so managers have devised endless, highly creative excuses to close shops when they would ordinarily be open. Sanitary Day, for instance, is a recently rediscovered requirement. Shops all over are closing for one day a month to clean and make the place, well, sanitary. Never before particularly fussy or fastidious, workers now take sufficient time off to scour the shop. When it reopens the next day, to no one's surprise, it looks exactly the same as before.

**page 233, top**

**MARCH 1992, Novokuznetsk, Siberia** That they have seen harder times than this does not make the current shortages any easier on them. They were stronger then, and had husbands.

**page 233, bottom**

**FEBRUARY 1992, Kutuzovsky Prospekt, Central Moscow** Prices will soon be decontrolled. People have bought even more shoes than usual, believing they can resell them soon for a profit, so the state shops are more empty looking than usual. In order to keep *all* goods from flying off the shelves, this sign has begun to appear in stores where "deficit" goods are found: "For Special Categories of the population: Veterans of The Great Patriotic War, Invalids, Afghan War Veterans, Chernobyl Victims, People made homeless by fire, and Newlyweds."

**pages 234–235**

**MAY 1991, Kubatli, Azerbaijan** A sixty-eight-year-old Armenian widow expelled by Azerbaijani police from her home in Ngorno-Karabakh, the autonomous Armenian enclave inside Azerbaijan, to a field here. She and two hundred fellow villagers were transported without their belongings to refugee housing in Yerevan, the Armenian capital.

**page 236**

**SEPTEMBER 1992** Khabarovsk Airport is the air transport hub of the Soviet Far East. Here, Russian and Ukrainian traders are en route from Harbin, Manchuria, to the European Soviet cities. With them are bundles of down coats and polyester shirts, cheap in China but scarce in the Union. They must wait a week or more in the air terminal for the chance to bribe their way onto a flight going West. Surprisingly, they do not grumble about the tedious wait; they are biding their time in one another's company, taking turns watching the goods, daydreaming of spending their earnings.

**page 237**

**FEBRUARY 1991, Novi Arbat (Kalaninsky Prospekt)** A new phenomenon on the streets of Moscow—beggars.

**page 238–241**

**AUGUST 19, 1991, Moscow** In an attempted coup d'état, eight plotters put Gorbachev under house arrest at his vacation dacha in the Crimea; Interior Ministry and KGB troops surrounded the Kremlin, and tanks rolled through the boulevards of Moscow, encircling the White House (the Soviet parliament). Watching the tanks move in, a woman screams her contempt at the troops, saying their mothers would be ashamed of them.

**pages 242–243**

**AUGUST 19, 1991, Moscow** At 6 P.M. on the day of the coup, the plotters held a press conference. It was a farce. Vice President Gennady I. Yanayev *(top)*, the group's titular leader, was plainly drunk. His hands shook, and journalists laughed out loud at his poorly contrived story of Gorbachev's "ill health" precipitating the coup. The masterminds, KGB chief Vladimir A. Kryuchkov and Interior Minister Boris H. Pugo *(bottom)*, were remorseless to the end. Kryuchkov was thrown in prison, and Pugo blew his brains out when the police came to arrest him.

**page 244, top, page 245, top**

**SEPTEMBER 1991** The Air Show at Kubinka Air Force Base near Moscow takes place on schedule. Soviet aircraft are competitive throughout the world, and the desperate need for hard currency assures that the show will go on.

**page 244, bottom**

**FEBRUARY 1991** A group of irregulars, the Tamarasheny local militia, hunting for Georgian troops near Tskvinhali, South Ossetia. They have been out all night in the hills; just at dawn, they come under fire from the hillside. There are no casualties.

**page 245, bottom**

**AUGUST 21, 1991, Moscow** People on the Garden Ring Road come out to congratulate loyal soldiers, who are going back to their barracks. With all remaining troops coming over to the government's side and the plotters arrested, the coup is finished.

**pages 246–247**

**OCTOBER 1991** While many Soviets have profound conflicts over Lenin and his meaning in their lives, they harbor no ambiguity about lesser lights in the Soviet pantheon. Immediately following the failed coup, the statue of Felix Dzerzhinski, Polish-born founder of the KGB, was disinstalled with great fanfare from its pedestal in front of KGB headquarters. Thousands cheered the symbolic hanging, as a steel cable was wrapped around the statue's neck and yanked by a heavy crane onto the back of a flatbed truck. The statues of Dzerzhinski and others—even a few Stalins—have been hauled to a spot across from Gorky Park, where they have all found useful employment as a playground for children.

**pages 248–249**

**FEBRUARY 1992, Ekaterinburg** Today is the dreaded day food prices are decontrolled, except for milk and bread, throughout most of the country. It is the first time these shoppers have ever seen a drastic price rise for staples like meat, sausage, eggs. Thus begins the "Big Bang" that Western economists prescribe for the Union's economic ills. For the second time in seventy-five years, Russians will have a completely new, mandatory economic idea forced upon them.

Brought up to believe that the state will provide, these people are learning that they are part of the experiment too. What magnifies their shock is that they live in Boris N. Yeltsin's hometown, where he was Party leader. They expected to be sheltered from the worst of reforms.

Today also marks the end of Yeltsin's honeymoon with his compatriots.

# Acknowledgments

Without the continued dedication and optimism of Marcel Saba, John F. Thornton, and David R. Metz, this book would not have come into being.

The photographs were made on assignment for *Der Spiegel*. Thanks to Dr. Romain Leick, Eva-Maria von Maydall, Josef Csallos, Monica Rick, Jörg-Reiner Mettke, Dr. Andrei Batrak, and Carlos Widmann.

At Yale University Press, thanks to Jonathan Brent, Paul Royster, Aileen Novick, Tamara Belknap, and Nicholas Raposo.

Thanks to: Sergei V. Korotkov, Tatiana N. Lukashevich, Asele A. Surina, Alexander I. Yefzemov, Dimitri D. Pleshkov, Janet DeJesus, Elizabeth LaGrua, Jean-François Leroy, Mark Pringle, Martin Colyer, Joseph Delora, Mike Newler, Chuck Westfall, Michel Rudman, Anne Collot, Rose Shoshana, Colin Jacobson, Glenn R. Mack, Patrick Robert, Lou Desiderio, Vladimir N. Penkin, J. C. Suares, Richard and Candace DiLello, Pierre Gassmann, Margot Klingsporn, Jessica D'Amico, Joe Spieler, Ada Muellner, Richard A. Bloom, Alain Nogues, Susan Gregg, Bill and Kathi Brodhead, Filip Horvat, Peter Howe, Pierre-Philippe Lob, Michael and Marian Newman, Steve Davis, Tony Rojas, Marc Osborn, Michael Croan, Bill Hannigan, Stafford Squire, Tami Rodabaugh, Kristina Lazsko, and Michael and Michelle Williamson.

*This book was made possible thanks to the support of Corbis and Canon USA.*

Photos edited by Alison Morley and Shepard Sherbell, assisted by Natasha O'Connor.
Book and jacket design by Sonia Shannon.
Text edited by Phillip King.
Silver gelatin prints by Voyan Mitrovic, Picto Paris-Montparnasse.
Digital translation by David Roseburg and Anne W. Taylor, Corbis, Bellevue, Washington.
Duotone separations from digital source by Guy Romagnoli and Michel Greppin, Entreprise d'arts graphiques Jean Genoud SA. Printing by Entreprise d'arts graphiques Jean Genoud SA, Lausanne, Switzerland, on Ikono Silk paper by Zanders Feinpapiere AG, Germany. Binding by Buchbinderei Schumacher AG, Schmitten, Switzerland.

Shepard Sherbell is represented by Corbis Saba, New York.

Library of Congress Catalog Card Number: 2001003264

A catalog record for this book is available from the British Library.

ISBN 0-300-09112-5

Printed in Switzerland

*www.sovietsbook.com*